POPE BENEDICT XVI

Christ Our Hope

THE PAPAL ADDRESSES OF THE APOSTOLIC JOURNEY TO THE UNITED STATES

Paulist Press
New York/Mahwah, NJ

Jacket and book design by Lynn Else
Jacket photographs by CNS photo/Nancy Wiechec

Library of Congress Cataloging-in-Publication Data is available upon request.

ISBN: 978-0-8091-0561-8

Published by Paulist Press
997 Macarthur Boulevard
Mahwah, New Jersey 07430

www.paulistpress.com

Printed and bound in the
United States of America

PUBLISHER'S INTRODUCTION TO THE WORDS OF POPE BENEDICT XVI

Reverend Lawrence Boadt, CSP

The visit of Pope Benedict XVI to the United States on April 15–20, 2008, was a momentous event for the American Catholic Church. Many American Catholics had thought that the Holy Father would not make plans to come to the United States, either because he was deeply engaged with efforts of renewal and re-evangelization of the Catholic faith in Europe, where the inroads of secularism have made great advances, or because he might find much protest and hostility to his visit in view of the strong feelings aroused by the clergy sexual abuse scandals of the last two decades. Then, when the planned visit was announced, others began to wonder whether the Pope intended to scold or lecture the American Church about such problems, or about Catholics in the United States being too-much affected by a spirit of individualism and making selective choices of what "Being Catholic" requires in doctrine and practice.

No such fears were ever realized. Instead, from the start, it was a trip filled with positive words and welcoming gestures of affection and support for the members of his Catholic family, who together make up the strongest national body of regularly practicing Catholics in the world. As he began his journey, he announced that he had wanted to come first of all so that he might celebrate with American Catholics the 200th anniversary of the founding of our first archdiocese in Baltimore, and the major dioceses of New York, Philadelphia, and Louisville, Kentucky. He also wished to address the United Nations, as had Popes Paul VI and John Paul II before him, on the need for universal human values and the dignity of all peoples, in a time that puts those very values to the test.

Although the Pope has often been cited as a warrior against the encroachment of secularism into European society, he instead constantly sounded the note of a hope-filled new evangelization, which he desired that his visit would reinvigorate and strengthen the living-out of the Gospel in American culture. Even before landing in Washington, D.C., he took the opportunity on his flight to praise the United States as the great idea and experiment: a secular society in which religion found a home to be free. He wasn't starry-eyed about American culture. He openly expressed his shame at the sexual abuse scandals that have affected the clergy and laity, he sympathized with the victims, and he promised effective and thoroughgoing reform so that such evil will not be able to happen again. But he also expressed constant optimism that America's pluralistic society can be a beacon for the future. As he said in his short address when welcomed by President Bush, he had come to visit "as a friend." Again and again, the word *hope* governed his confidence in the future of the Church. This theme of hope set the tone at each place he stopped: with educators, prelates, the young, the physically challenged, priests and religious, the large Masses for the faithful, and the members of other faiths, including the Jews of a synagogue founded by a survivor of the Holocaust. Everywhere he was warmly received, and in turn radiated warmth of affection and praise for every group with whom he met.

Paulist Press has prepared this volume with the same affection and gratitude for the Holy Father's visit to New York and Washington, which has coincided with the Paulist Fathers' celebration of their 150th year as a religious order, founded to evangelize American culture. A hundred and fifty years ago, in 1858, Pope Pius IX, who also expressed very positive attitudes to the United States, set Father Isaac Thomas Hecker and his Redemptorist colleagues apart as a new religious order that they might dedicate their missionary work to enhancing and enriching the Catholic presence and voice in North America. One of the special characteristics of Father Hecker's approach to evangelization was to make known the spiritual riches of Catholicism and its doctrine to the unique character of American democracy, and in turn to interpret America's particular values and dreams to the older and less democratic Catholicism found in Europe and even Rome.

Also during this 150th anniversary year, the archbishop of New York, Cardinal Edward Egan, has begun the process of proposing the Paulist founder, Father Hecker, as a candidate for sainthood and a model of an American spirituality. So, filled with the same hope and joy expressed by Pope Benedict XVI, Paulist Press offers this small book as a wonderful resource for building the bases of a vibrant new evangelization of hope for the American Church.

Lawrence Boadt, CSP

APOSTOLIC JOURNEY OF HIS HOLINESS BENEDICT XVI TO THE UNITED STATES OF AMERICA AND HIS VISIT TO THE UNITED NATIONS HEADQUARTERS

APRIL 15-21, 2008

PROGRAM

Italy

Tuesday, April 15, 2008

FIUMICINO (Rome)

12.00 Departure by plane from the Airport of Rome/Fiumicino for Washington/Andrews Air Force Base

INTERVIEW WITH THE HOLY FATHER DURING THE FLIGHT TO THE UNITED STATES OF AMERICA   1

United States of America

ANDREWS AIR FORCE BASE (Washington, D.C.)

16.00 Arrival at the Airport of the Andrews Air Force Base

Private welcoming by the President of the United States of America and the First Lady at the Airport of the Andrews Air Force Base

16.15 Transfer by car from the Airport of the Andrews Air Force Base to the Apostolic Nunciature of Washington

Washington, D.C.

Wednesday, April 16, 2008

Private Mass at the Chapel of the Apostolic Nunciature of Washington

10.10 Transfer by car from the Apostolic Nunciature to the White House

10.30 Welcoming ceremony on the South Lawn of the White House
ADDRESS OF THE HOLY FATHER 9

Courtesy visit to the President of the United States of America in the Oval Office of the White House
JOINT STATEMENT BETWEEN THE HOLY SEE AND THE UNITED STATES OF AMERICA 13

12.00 Transfer by Pope-mobile from the White House to the Apostolic Nunciature

13.00 Luncheon with the Cardinals of the United States of America, with the *Praesidium* of the United States Conference of Catholic Bishops *(USCCB)* and with the Papal Entourage at the Apostolic Nunciature

16.45 Greetings by various Catholic charitable foundations at the Apostolic Nunciature

17.00 Transfer by car from the Apostolic Nunciature to the National Shrine of the Immaculate Conception. Transfer from car to Pope-mobile

17.45 Celebration of Vespers and meeting with the Bishops of the United States of America at the National Shrine of the Immaculate Conception
ADDRESS OF THE HOLY FATHER 15

19.30 Transfer by car from the National Shrine of the Immaculate Conception to the Apostolic Nunciature

Thursday, April 17, 2008

9.00 Transfer by car from the Apostolic Nunciature to Nationals Park

10.00 Holy Mass at Nationals Park

12.15 Transfer by car from Nationals Park to the Apostolic Nunciature

16.40 Transfer by car from the Apostolic Nunciature to the Catholic University of America

17.00 Meeting with Catholic educators at the Conference Hall of the Catholic University of America

18.15 Transfer by Pope-mobile from the Catholic University of America to the Pope John Paul II Cultural Center of Washington

18.30 Meeting with representatives of other religions at the "Rotunda" Hall of the Pope John Paul II Cultural Center of Washington

19.30 Transfer by car from the Pope John Paul II Cultural Center to the Apostolic Nunciature

Friday, April 18, 2008

Private Mass at the Chapel of the Apostolic Nunciature in Washington

7.50 Farewell from the Apostolic Nunciature in Washington

8.00 Transfer by car from the Apostolic Nunciature to the airport of the Andrews Air Force Base in Washington

New York

9.45 Arrival at John Fitzgerald Kennedy International Airport of New York

10.00 Transfer by helicopter to Manhattan

10.30 Arrival at the heliport of Wall Street in Manhattan (New York). Transfer by car from the heliport of Wall Street to the Headquarters of the United Nations in New York

10.45 Visit to the United Nations Organization Headquarters

13.45 Transfer by car from the United Nations Headquarters to the Residence of the Permanent Observer to the United Nations

17:00 Transfer by car from the Papal Residence to Park East Synagogue

17:40 Transfer by car from Park East Synagogue to the Church of St. Joseph in New York

18.00 Ecumenical Prayer Service at the Parish of St. Joseph

19.15 Transfer by car from the Church of St. Joseph to the Papal Residence in New York

19.30 Dinner with the Cardinals of the United States of America, with the *Praesidium* of the United States Conference of Catholic Bishops *(USCCB)* and with the Papal Entourage at the Papal Residence in New York

Saturday, April 19, 2008

8.45 Transfer by car from the Papal Residence to St. Patrick's Cathedral

9.15 Holy Mass with priests, men and women religious in St. Patrick's Cathedral

11.30 Transfer on foot from St. Patrick's Cathedral to the Residence of the Archbishop of New York

12.00 Luncheon with the Bishops of the Archdiocese of New York and the Papal Entourage

13.15 Transfer by Pope-mobile from the Residence of the Archbishop to the Papal Residence in New York

16.00 Transfer by car from the Papal Residence to St. Joseph's Seminary in Yonkers, New York

16.30 Meeting with young people and seminarians at St. Joseph's Seminary in Yonkers, New York

18.30 Transfer by car from St. Joseph's Seminary to the Papal Residence in New York

Sunday, April 20, 2008

9.10 Transfer by car from the Papal Residence to Ground Zero

9.30 Visit to Ground Zero
PRAYER OF THE HOLY FATHER   117

10.00 Transfer by car from Ground Zero to the Papal Residence in New York

13.50 Transfer by car from the Papal Residence to Yankee Stadium in Bronx, New York

14.30 Holy Mass at Yankee Stadium
HOMILY OF THE HOLY FATHER   119

16.45 Transfer by car from Yankee Stadium to the Papal Residence in New York

19.00 Transfer by car from the Papal Residence to the heliport of Wall Street

19.20 Arrival at the heliport of Wall Street

19.30 Transfer by helicopter from the heliport of Wall Street to John Fitzgerald Kennedy International Airport of New York

20.00 Arrival at John Fitzgerald Kennedy International Airport
FAREWELL CEREMONY   127

20.30 Departure by plane from John Fitzgerald Kennedy International Airport of New York for Rome

Italy

Monday, April 21, 2008

ROME/CIAMPINO
10.45 Arrival at Rome/Ciampino Airport

CONTENTS

INTERVIEW WITH THE HOLY FATHER BENEDICT XVI DURING THE FLIGHT TO THE UNITED STATES OF AMERICA

Tuesday, April 15, 2008

Fr. Lombardi: *Welcome, Your Holiness! In the name of all my colleagues present, I thank you for your gracious availability in giving us suggestions and ideas for reporting on this Journey. It is your second intercontinental Trip: your first as Pope to America, to the United States and to the United Nations. It is an important and eagerly—awaited Visit. To begin with, could you tell us something about how you feel, the hopes you have for this Journey and what is its fundamental goal from your viewpoint?*

The Holy Father: My Journey has two goals in particular. The first is to visit the Church in America, in the United States. There is one special reason for it: 200 years ago Baltimore was raised to a Metropolitan See and at the same time four other new Dioceses came into being: New York, Philadelphia, Boston and Louisville. Thus, it is a great Jubilee for this core of the Church in the United States, a time of reflection on the past and above all of reflection on the future, on how to respond to the great challenges of our time,

1

in the present and in view of the future. And naturally, inter-religious and ecumenical meetings are part of this Visit, especially an additional Meeting in the Synagogue with our Jewish friends on the eve of their Passover Feast. This is, therefore, the religious and pastoral aspect of the Church in the United States at this moment in our history, and the Meeting with all the others in this common brotherhood that binds us in a common responsibility. At this time I would also like to thank President Bush who will be at the airport to meet me and set aside a lot of time for conversation, besides receiving me on my birthday. The second goal is the Visit to the United Nations. Here too there is a special reason: 60 years have passed since the Universal Declaration of Human Rights. This is the anthropological basis, the philosophy, on which the United Nations stands, the human and spiritual foundations on which it is built. Thus, it is truly a time for reflection, the time to resume awareness of this important stage in history. Various different cultural traditions converged in the Declaration of Human Rights, above all, an anthropology that recognizes man as a subject of rights preceding all institutions, with common values to be respected by all. This Visit, which is taking place precisely at the moment of a crisis in values, therefore seems to me to be important in order to reconfirm together that everything began at that moment and to recover it for our future.

Fr. Lombardi: *Let us now move on to the questions that you presented in the past few days and that some of you will present to the Holy Father. Let us begin with the question of John Allen, whom I do not think needs to be introduced since he is a very well-known commentator on Vatican affairs in the United States.*

Holy Father, I am asking the question in English, if I may, and perhaps, if it were possible, if we could have a sen-

tence or a word in English we would be very grateful. This is the question: the Church you will find in the United States is a large Church, a lively Church, but also a suffering Church, in a certain sense, especially because of the recent crisis caused by sexual abuse. The American People are expecting a word from you, a message from you on this crisis. What will be your Message for this suffering Church?

The Holy Father (in English): It is a great suffering for the Church in the United States and for the Church in general, for me personally, that this could happen. If I read the history of these events, it is difficult for me to understand how it was possible for priests to fail in this way in the mission to give healing, to give God's love to these children. I am ashamed and we will do everything possible to ensure that this does not happen in future. I think we have to act on three levels: the first is at the level of justice and the political level. I will not speak at this moment about homosexuality: this is another thing. We will absolutely exclude pedophiles from the sacred ministry; it is absolutely incompatible, and whoever is really guilty of being a pedophile cannot be a priest. So at this first level we can do justice and help the victims, because they are deeply affected; these are the two sides of justice: one, that pedophiles cannot be priests and the other, to help in any possible way the victims. Then there is a pastoral level. The victims will need healing and help and assistance and reconciliation: this is a big pastoral engagement and I know that the Bishops and the priests and all Catholic people in the United States will do whatever possible to help, to assist, to heal. We have made a visitation of the seminaries and we will do all that is possible in the education of seminarians for a deep spiritual, human and intellectual formation for the students. Only sound persons can be admitted to the priesthood and only persons with a deep personal life in Christ and who have a deep sacramental life. So, I know that the Bishops and directors of seminarians will do all possible to have a strong, strong discernment because it is more important to have good priests than to have many priests. This is also our third level, and we hope that we can do, and have done and will do in the future, all that is possible to heal these wounds.

Fr. Lombardi: *Thank you, Your Holiness. Our colleagues sent in many questions on the subject of immigration, on the presence of Spanish—speaking people in American society. Journalist Andrés Leonardo Beltramo Alvares, who works for the Mexican News Agency, asks about this.*

Your Holiness, I am asking the question in Italian and then, if you wish, you can make your comment in Spanish— a greeting, only a greeting! There is enormous growth in the Hispanic presence in the Church of the United States in general: the Catholic community is becoming more and more bilingual and almost bicultural. At the same time, there is an increasing anti—immigration movement in society: the situation of immigrants is marked by forms of precariousness and discrimination. Is it your intention to speak of this problem and to ask America to give a warm welcome to immigrants, many of whom are Catholic?

The Holy Father: I cannot speak Spanish but *mis saludos y mi bendición para todos los hispánicos.* Of course, I will be speaking about this point. I have had various *ad limina* visits from Bishops of Central America and also from South America, and I have seen the breadth of this problem, especially the serious problem of the break—up of families. And this is really dangerous for the social, moral and human fabric of these Countries. However, it is necessary to distinguish between measures to be taken straight away and long-term solutions. The fundamental solution is that there should no longer be any need to emigrate because there are sufficient jobs in the homeland, a self-sufficient social fabric, so that there is no longer any need to emigrate. Therefore, we must all work to achieve this goal and for a social development that makes it possible to offer citizens work and a future in their homeland. And I would also like to speak to the President on this point, because it is above all the United States that must help these countries to develop. It is in everyone's interests, not only these countries but of the world and also of the United States. Then, short-term measures: it is very important to help families in particular. In the light of the conversations I have had with Bishops about the main problems, it appears that families should be protected rather than destroyed. What can be done should be done. Of course, it is also necessary to do everything possible to prevent precariousness and every kind of violence, and to help so that they may really have a dignified life wherever they may be. I also want to say that there are many problems, much suffering, but also such great hospitality! I know that the American Bishops' Conference in particular works closely with the Latin American Bishops' Conferences with a view to necessary aid. Besides all the painful things, let us not forget the great and true humanity, the many positive actions that also exist.

Fr. Lombardi: *Thank you, Your Holiness. Now a question that refers to American society and, to be precise, to the place of religious values in American society. Let us give the floor to our colleague Andrea Tornielli, who is on the Vatican desk of an Italian newspaper.*

Holy Father, in receiving the new Ambassador of the United States of America, you noted that the public "values the role of religious belief in ensuring a sound democratic order" in the United States. I wanted to ask you if you consider this a plausible model for a secularized Europe too, or

whether you think there can also be the risk that religion and
God's Name could be used as a vehicle for certain policies,
even war.

The Holy Father: Of course, in Europe we cannot simply
copy the United States: we have our own history. But we
must all learn from one another. What I find fascinating in
the United States is that they began with a positive concept
of secularity, because this new people was composed of communities and individuals who had fled from the State Church
and wanted to have a lay, a secular State that would give
access and opportunities to all denominations, to all forms of
religious practice. Thus, an intentionally secular new State
was born; they were opposed to a State Church. But the State
itself had to be secular precisely out of love for religion in its
authenticity, which can only be lived freely. And thus, we find
this situation of a State deliberately and decidedly secular but
precisely through a religious will in order to give authenticity to religion. And we know that in studying America,
Alexis de Toqueville noticed that secular institutions live with
a de facto moral consensus that exists among the citizens.
This seems to me to be a fundamental and positive model. It
should be taken into account that in Europe in the meantime,
over 200 years have passed with many developments. Today,
there is also in the United States the attack of a new secularism, quite a different kind. Whereas, at first the problems
concerned immigration, but later in the course of history the
situation became complicated and therefore differentiated.
But the foundation, the fundamental model also seems to me
today to be worthy of being borne in mind in Europe.

Fr. Lombardi: *Thank you, Your Holiness. And now, a last*
topic that concerns your Visit to the United Nations, and the
question about this is asked by John Pavis, who is in charge

of the [Rome branch of] the Catholic News Agency of the United States.

Holy Father, the Pope is often considered to be humanity's conscience and for this reason too, his Discourse to the United Nations is very much anticipated. I would like to ask: Do you think that a multilateral institution like the United Nations can safeguard the principles of the Catholic Church deemed "non-negotiable", that is, the principles founded on natural law?

The Holy Father: The fundamental objective of the United Nations is precisely this: that it safeguard the common values of humanity, on which is based the peaceful coexistence of nations, the observance of justice and the development of justice. I mentioned briefly that I think it very important that the United Nations be founded precisely on the idea of human rights, rights that express non-negotiable values, that precede all the institutions and constitute the foundations of all the institutions. And it is important that this should be the convergence between the cultures that have achieved consensus on the fact that these values are fundamental, that they are engraved in man's very being. It is important to renew this knowledge that the United Nations, with its peacekeeping role, can only work if it is based on common values that are subsequently expressed in "rights" that must be observed by all. To confirm this fundamental concept and to bring it as current as possible is an objective of my mission. Lastly, since at the outset Fr, Lombardi also asked me a question about my feelings, I would like to say that I am going most joyfully to the United States! I have previously visited the U.S. several times, I know this great Country, I know the great vivacity of the Church despite all the problems, and I am happy to be able to meet this great People and this great Church at this historical moment for both the Church and the United Nations. Thank you to all!

ADDRESS OF
HIS HOLINESS BENEDICT XVI
AT THE WELCOMING CEREMONY

SOUTH LAWN OF THE WHITE HOUSE, WASHINGTON, D.C.
Wednesday, April 16, 2008

MR. PRESIDENT,

Thank you for your gracious words of welcome on behalf of the people of the United States of America. I deeply appreciate your invitation to visit this great country. My visit coincides with an important moment in the life of the Catholic community in America: the celebration of the two-hundredth anniversary of the elevation of the country's first Diocese—Baltimore—to a metropolitan Archdiocese, and the establishment of the Sees of New York, Boston, Philadelphia and Louisville. Yet I am happy to be here as a guest of all Americans. I come as a friend, a preacher of the Gospel and one with great respect for this vast pluralistic society. America's Catholics have made, and continue to make, an excellent contribution to the life of their country. As I begin my visit, I trust that my presence will be a source of renewal and hope for the Church in the United States, and strengthen the resolve of Catholics to contribute ever more responsibly to the life of this nation, of which they are proud to be citizens.

From the dawn of the Republic, America's quest for freedom has been guided by the conviction that the principles governing political and social life are intimately linked to a moral order based on the dominion of God the Creator. The framers of this nation's founding documents drew upon this conviction when they proclaimed the "self-evident truth" that all men are created equal and endowed with inalienable rights grounded in the laws of nature and of nature's God. The course of American history demonstrates the difficulties, the struggles, and the great intellectual and moral resolve which were demanded to shape a society which faithfully embodied these noble principles. In that process, which forged the soul of the nation, religious beliefs were a constant inspiration and driving force, as for example in the struggle against slavery and in the civil rights movement. In our time too, particularly in moments of crisis, Americans continue to find their strength in a commitment to this patrimony of shared ideals and aspirations.

In the next few days, I look forward to meeting not only with America's Catholic community, but with other Christian communities and representatives of the many religious traditions present in this country. Historically, not only Catholics, but all believers have found here the freedom to worship God in accordance with the dictates of their conscience, while at the same time being accepted as part of a commonwealth in which each individual and group can make its voice heard. As the nation faces the increasingly complex political and ethical issues of our time, I am confident that the American people will find in their religious beliefs a precious source of insight and an inspiration to pursue reasoned, responsible and respectful dialogue in the effort to build a more humane and free society.

Freedom is not only a gift, but also a summons to personal responsibility. Americans know this from experience—almost every town in this country has its monuments honoring those who sacrificed their lives in defense of freedom, both at home and abroad. The preservation of freedom calls for the cultivation of virtue, self-discipline, sacrifice for the common good and a sense of responsibility towards the less fortunate. It also demands the courage to engage in civic life and to bring one's deepest beliefs and values to reasoned public debate. In a word, freedom is ever new. It is a challenge held out to each generation, and it must constantly be won over for the cause of good (cf. *Spe Salvi*, 24). Few have understood this as clearly as the late Pope John Paul II. In reflecting on the spiritual victory of freedom over totalitarianism in his native Poland and in eastern Europe, he reminded us that history shows, time and again, that "in a world without truth, freedom loses its foundation", and a democracy without values can lose its very soul (cf. *Centesimus Annus*, 46). Those prophetic words in some sense echo the conviction of President Washington, expressed in his Farewell Address, that religion and morality represent "indispensable supports" of political prosperity.

The Church, for her part, wishes to contribute to building a world ever more worthy of the human person, created in the image and likeness of God (cf. *Gen* 1:26–27). She is convinced that faith sheds new light on all things, and that the Gospel reveals the noble vocation and sublime destiny of every man and woman (cf. *Gaudium et Spes*, 10). Faith also gives us the strength to respond to our high calling, and the hope that inspires us to work for an ever more just and fraternal society. Democracy can only flourish, as your founding fathers realized, when political leaders and those whom they represent are guided by truth and bring the wisdom born of firm moral principle to decisions affecting the life and future of the nation.

For well over a century, the United States of America has played an important role in the international community. On Friday, God willing, I will have the honor of addressing the United Nations Organization, where I hope to encourage the efforts under way to make that institution an ever more effective voice for the legitimate aspirations of all the world's peoples. On this, the sixtieth anniversary of the Universal Declaration of Human Rights, the need for global solidarity is as urgent as ever, if all people are to live in a way worthy of their dignity—as brothers and sisters dwelling in the same house and around that table which God's bounty has set for all his children. America has traditionally shown herself generous in meeting immediate human needs, fostering development and offering relief to the victims of natural catastrophes. I am confident that this concern for the greater human family will continue to find expression in support for the patient efforts of international diplomacy to resolve conflicts and promote progress. In this way, coming generations will be able to live in a world where truth, freedom and justice can flourish—a world where the God-given dignity and rights of every man, woman and child are cherished, protected and effectively advanced.

Mr. President, dear friends: as I begin my visit to the United States, I express once more my gratitude for your invitation, my joy to be in your midst, and my fervent prayers that Almighty God will confirm this nation and its people in the ways of justice, prosperity and peace. God bless America!

JOINT STATEMENT BETWEEN THE HOLY SEE AND THE UNITED STATES OF AMERICA

OVAL OFFICE OF THE WHITE HOUSE
Wednesday, April 16, 2008

At the end of the private meeting between the Holy Father Benedict XVI and U.S. President George W. Bush, the Holy See and the Office of the President of the United States of America released a joint declaration:

President Bush, on behalf of all Americans, welcomed the Holy Father, wished him a happy birthday, and thanked him for the spiritual and moral guidance, which he offers to the whole human family. The President wished the Pope every success in his *Apostolic Journey* and in his address at the United Nations, and expressed appreciation for the Pope's upcoming visit to "Ground Zero" in New York.

During their meeting, the Holy Father and the President discussed a number of topics of common interest to the Holy See and the United States of America, including moral and religious considerations to which both parties are committed: the respect of the dignity of the human person; the defense and promotion of life, matrimony and the family; the education of future generations; human rights and religious freedom; sustainable development and the struggle against poverty and pandemics, especially in Africa. In regard to the latter, the Holy Father welcomed the United States' substantial financial contributions in this area. The two reaffirmed their total rejection of terrorism as well as the manipulation of religion to justify immoral and violent acts against innocents. They further touched on the need to confront terrorism with appropriate means that respect the human person and his or her rights.

The Holy Father and the President devoted considerable time in their discussions to the Middle East, in particular resolving the Israel-Palestinian conflict in line with the vision of two states living side-by-side in peace and security, their mutual support for the sovereignty and independence of Lebanon, and their common concern for the situation in Iraq and particularly the precarious state of Christian communities there and elsewhere in the region. The Holy Father and the President expressed hope for an end to violence and for a prompt and comprehensive solution to the crises which afflict the region.

The Holy Father and the President also considered the situation in Latin America with reference, among other matters, to immigrants, and the need for a coordinated policy regarding immigration, especially their humane treatment and the well being of their families.

ADDRESS OF
HIS HOLINESS BENEDICT XVI
TO THE BISHOPS OF THE
UNITED STATES OF AMERICA

NATIONAL SHRINE OF THE IMMACULATE
CONCEPTION IN WASHINGTON, D.C.
Wednesday, April 16, 2008

DEAR BROTHER BISHOPS,

It gives me great joy to greet you today, at the start of my visit to this country, and I thank Cardinal George for the gracious words he has addressed to me on your behalf. I want to thank all of you, especially the Officers of the Episcopal Conference, for the hard work that has gone into the preparation of this visit. My grateful appreciation goes also to the staff and volunteers of the National Shrine, who have welcomed us here this evening. American Catholics are noted for their loyal devotion to the see of Peter. My pastoral visit here is an opportunity to strengthen further the bonds of communion that unite us. We began by celebrating Evening Prayer in this Basilica dedicated to the Immaculate Conception of the Blessed Virgin Mary, a shrine of special significance to American Catholics, right in the heart of your capital city.

15

Gathered in prayer with Mary, Mother of Jesus, we lovingly commend to our heavenly Father the people of God in every part of the United States.

For the Catholic communities of Boston, New York, Philadelphia and Louisville, this is a year of particular celebration, as it marks the bicentenary of the establishment of these local Churches as Dioceses. I join you in giving thanks for the many graces granted to the Church there during these two centuries. As this year also marks the bicentenary of the elevation of the founding see of Baltimore to an Archdiocese, it gives me an opportunity to recall with admiration and gratitude the life and ministry of John Carroll, the first Bishop of Baltimore—a worthy leader of the Catholic community in your newly independent nation. His tireless efforts to spread the Gospel in the vast territory under his care laid the foundations for the ecclesial life of your country and enabled the Church in America to grow to maturity. Today the Catholic community you serve is one of the largest in the world, and one of the most influential. How important it is, then, to let your light so shine before your fellow citizens and before the world, "that they may see your good works and give glory to your Father who is in heaven" (*Matt* 5:16).

Many of the people to whom John Carroll and his fellow Bishops were ministering two centuries ago had traveled from distant lands. The diversity of their origins is reflected in the rich variety of ecclesial life in present-day America. Brother Bishops, I want to encourage you and your communities to continue to welcome the immigrants who join your ranks today, to share their joys and hopes, to support them in their sorrows and trials, and to help them flourish in their new home. This, indeed, is what your fellow countrymen have done for generations. From the beginning, they have opened their doors to the tired, the poor, the "huddled masses yearning to breathe free" (cf. *Sonnet inscribed on the*

Statue of Liberty). These are the people whom America has made her own.

Of those who came to build a new life here, many were able to make good use of the resources and opportunities that they found, and to attain a high level of prosperity. Indeed, the people of this country are known for their great vitality and creativity. They are also known for their generosity. After the attack on the Twin Towers in September 2001, and again after Hurricane Katrina in 2005, Americans displayed their readiness to come to the aid of their brothers and sisters in need. On the international level, the contribution made by the people of America to relief and rescue operations after the tsunami of December 2004 is a further illustration of this compassion. Let me express my particular appreciation for the many forms of humanitarian assistance provided by American Catholics through Catholic Charities and other agencies. Their generosity has borne fruit in the care shown to the poor and needy, and in the energy that has gone into building the nationwide network of Catholic parishes, hospitals, schools and universities. All of this gives great cause for thanksgiving.

America is also a land of great faith. Your people are remarkable for their religious fervor and they take pride in belonging to a worshipping community. They have confidence in God, and they do not hesitate to bring moral arguments rooted in biblical faith into their public discourse. Respect for freedom of religion is deeply ingrained in the American consciousness—a fact which has contributed to this country's attraction for generations of immigrants, seeking a home where they can worship freely in accordance with their beliefs.

In this connection, I happily acknowledge the presence among you of Bishops from all the venerable Eastern Churches in communion with the Successor of Peter, whom I greet with

special joy. Dear Brothers, I ask you to assure your communities of my deep affection and my continued prayers, both
for them and for the many brothers and sisters who remain
in their land of origin. Your presence here is a reminder of
the courageous witness to Christ of so many members of
your communities, often amid suffering, in their respective
homelands. It is also a great enrichment of the ecclesial life of
America, giving vivid expression to the Church's catholicity
and the variety of her liturgical and spiritual traditions.

It is in this fertile soil, nourished from so many different
sources, that all of you, Brother Bishops, are called to sow
the seeds of the Gospel today. This leads me to ask how, in
the twenty-first century, a bishop can best fulfill the call to
"make all things new in Christ, our hope"? How can he lead
his people to "an encounter with the living God", the source
of that life-transforming hope of which the Gospel speaks (cf.
Spe Salvi, 4)?

Perhaps he needs to begin by clearing away some of the
barriers to such an encounter. While it is true that this country is marked by a genuinely religious spirit, the subtle influence of secularism can nevertheless color the way people
allow their faith to influence their behavior. Is it consistent to
profess our beliefs in church on Sunday, and then during the
week to promote business practices or medical procedures
contrary to those beliefs? Is it consistent for practicing
Catholics to ignore or exploit the poor and the marginalized,
to promote sexual behavior contrary to Catholic moral
teaching, or to adopt positions that contradict the right to
life of every human being from conception to natural death?
Any tendency to treat religion as a private matter must be
resisted. Only when their faith permeates every aspect of
their lives do Christians become truly open to the transforming power of the Gospel.

For an affluent society, a further obstacle to an encounter with the living God lies in the subtle influence of materialism, which can all too easily focus the attention on the hundredfold, which God promises now in this time, at the expense of the eternal life which he promises in the age to come (cf. *Mark* 10:30). People today need to be reminded of the ultimate purpose of their lives. They need to recognize that implanted within them is a deep thirst for God. They need to be given opportunities to drink from the wells of his infinite love. It is easy to be entranced by the almost unlimited possibilities that science and technology place before us; it is easy to make the mistake of thinking we can obtain by our own efforts the fulfillment of our deepest needs. This is an illusion. Without God, who alone bestows upon us what we by ourselves cannot attain (cf. *Spe Salvi,* 31), our lives are ultimately empty. People need to be constantly reminded to cultivate a relationship with him who came that we might have life in abundance (cf. *John* 10:10). The goal of all our pastoral and catechetical work, the object of our preaching, and the focus of our sacramental ministry should be to help people establish and nurture that living relationship with "Christ Jesus, our hope" (1 *Tim* 1:1).

In a society which values personal freedom and autonomy, it is easy to lose sight of our dependence on others as well as the responsibilities that we bear towards them. This emphasis on individualism has even affected the Church (cf. *Spe Salvi,* 13–15), giving rise to a form of piety which sometimes emphasizes our private relationship with God at the expense of our calling to be members of a redeemed community. Yet from the beginning, God saw that "it is not good for man to be alone" (*Gen* 2:18). We were created as social beings who find fulfillment only in love—for God and for our neighbor. If we are truly to gaze upon him who is the source of our joy, we need to do so as members of the people of God (cf. *Spe Salvi,* 14). If this seems counter-cultural, that is simply further evidence of the urgent need for a renewed evangelization of culture.

Here in America, you are blessed with a Catholic laity of considerable cultural diversity, who place their wide-ranging gifts at the service of the Church and of society at large. They look to you to offer them encouragement, leadership and direction. In an age that is saturated with information, the importance of providing sound formation in the faith cannot be overstated. American Catholics have traditionally placed a high value on religious education, both in schools and in the context of adult formation programs. These need to be maintained and expanded. The many generous men and women who devote themselves to charitable activity need to be helped to renew their dedication through a "formation of the heart": an "encounter with God in Christ which awakens their love and opens their spirits to others" (*Deus Caritas Est,* 31). At a time when advances in medical science bring new hope to many, they also give rise to previously unimagined ethical challenges. This makes it more important than ever to offer thorough formation in the Church's moral teaching to Catholics engaged in health care. Wise guidance is needed in all these apostolates, so that they may bear abundant fruit; if they are truly to promote the integral good of the human person, they too need to be made new in Christ our hope.

As preachers of the Gospel and leaders of the Catholic community, you are also called to participate in the exchange of ideas in the public square, helping to shape cultural attitudes. In a context where free speech is valued, and where vigorous and honest debate is encouraged, yours is a respected voice that has much to offer to the discussion of the pressing social and moral questions of the day. By ensuring that the Gospel is clearly heard, you not only form the people of your own community, but in view of the global reach of mass communication, you help to spread the message of Christian hope throughout the world.

Clearly, the Church's influence on public debate takes place on many different levels. In the United States, as elsewhere, there is much current and proposed legislation that gives cause for concern from the point of view of morality, and the Catholic community, under your guidance, needs to offer a clear and united witness on such matters. Even more important, though, is the gradual opening of the minds and hearts of the wider community to moral truth. Here much remains to be done. Crucial in this regard is the role of the lay faithful to act as a "leaven" in society. Yet it cannot be assumed that all Catholic citizens think in harmony with the Church's teaching on today's key ethical questions. Once again, it falls to you to ensure that the moral formation provided at every level of ecclesial life reflects the authentic teaching of the Gospel of life.

In this regard, a matter of deep concern to us all is the state of the family within society. Indeed, Cardinal George mentioned earlier that you have included the strengthening of marriage and family life among the priorities for your attention over the next few years. In this year's *World Day of Peace Message* I spoke of the essential contribution that healthy family life makes to peace within and between nations. In the family home we experience "some of the fundamental elements of peace: justice and love between brothers and sisters, the role of authority expressed by parents, loving concern for the members who are weaker because of youth, sickness or old age, mutual help in the necessities of life, readiness to accept others and, if necessary, to forgive them" (no. 3). The family is also the primary place for evangelization, for passing on the faith, for helping young people to appreciate the importance of religious practice and Sunday observance. How can we not be dismayed as we observe the sharp decline of the family as a basic element of Church and society? Divorce and infidelity have increased, and many young men and women are choosing to postpone marriage or to forego it altogether. To some young Catholics, the sacramental bond of marriage seems scarcely distinguishable from a civil bond, or even a purely informal and open-ended arrangement to live with another person. Hence we have an alarming decrease in the number of Catholic marriages in the United States together with an increase in cohabitation, in which the Christ-like mutual self-giving of spouses, sealed by a public promise to live out the demands of an indissoluble lifelong commitment, is simply absent. In such circumstances, children are denied the secure environment that they need in order truly to flourish as human beings, and society is denied the stable building blocks which it requires if the cohesion and moral focus of the community are to be maintained.

As my predecessor, Pope John Paul II taught, "The person principally responsible in the Diocese for the pastoral care of the family is the Bishop...he must devote to it personal interest, care, time, personnel and resources, but above all personal support for the families and for all those who... assist him in the pastoral care of the family" (*Familiaris Consortio,* 73). It is your task to proclaim boldly the arguments from faith and reason in favor of the institution of marriage, understood as a lifelong commitment between a man and a woman, open to the transmission of life. This message should resonate with people today, because it is essentially an unconditional and unreserved "yes" to life, a "yes" to love, and a "yes" to the aspirations at the heart of our common humanity, as we strive to fulfill our deep yearning for intimacy with others and with the Lord.

Among the countersigns to the Gospel of life found in America and elsewhere is one that causes deep shame: the sexual abuse of minors. Many of you have spoken to me of the enormous pain that your communities have suffered when clerics have betrayed their priestly obligations and duties by such gravely immoral behavior. As you strive to eliminate this evil wherever it occurs, you may be assured of the prayerful support of God's people throughout the world. Rightly, you attach priority to showing compassion and care to the victims. It is your God-given responsibility as pastors to bind up the wounds caused by every breach of trust, to foster healing, to promote reconciliation and to reach out with loving concern to those so seriously wronged.

Responding to this situation has not been easy and, as the President of your Episcopal Conference has indicated, it was "sometimes very badly handled". Now that the scale and gravity of the problem is more clearly understood, you have been able to adopt more focused remedial and disciplinary measures and to promote a safe environment that gives greater protection to young people. While it must be remembered that the overwhelming majority of clergy and religious in America do outstanding work in bringing the liberating message of the Gospel to the people entrusted to their care, it is vitally important that the vulnerable always be shielded from those who would cause harm. In this regard, your efforts to heal and protect are bearing great fruit not only for those directly under your pastoral care, but for all of society.

If they are to achieve their full purpose, however, the policies and programs you have adopted need to be placed in a wider context. Children deserve to grow up with a healthy understanding of sexuality and its proper place in human relationships. They should be spared the degrading manifestations and the crude manipulation of sexuality so prevalent today. They have a right to be educated in authentic moral values rooted in the dignity of the human person. This brings us back to our consideration of the centrality of the family and the need to promote the Gospel of life. What does it mean to speak of child protection when pornography and violence can be viewed in so many homes through media widely available today? We need to reassess urgently the values underpinning society, so that a sound moral formation can be offered to young people and adults alike. All have a part to play in this task—not only parents, religious leaders, teachers and catechists, but the media and entertainment industries as well. Indeed, every member of society can contribute to this moral renewal and benefit from it. Truly caring about young people and the future of our civilization means recognizing our responsibility to promote and live by the authentic moral values which alone enable the human person to flourish. It falls to you, as pastors modeled upon Christ, the Good Shepherd, to proclaim this message loud and clear, and thus to address the sin of abuse within the wider context of sexual *mores*. Moreover, by acknowledging and confronting the problem when it occurs in an ecclesial setting, you can give a lead to others, since this scourge is found not only within your Dioceses, but in every sector of society. It calls for a determined, collective response.

Priests, too, need your guidance and closeness during this difficult time. They have experienced shame over what has occurred, and there are those who feel they have lost some of the trust and esteem they once enjoyed. Not a few are experiencing a closeness to Christ in his Passion as they struggle to come to terms with the consequences of the crisis. The Bishop, as father, brother and friend of his priests, can help them to draw spiritual fruit from this union with Christ by making them aware of the Lord's consoling presence in the midst of their suffering, and by encouraging them to walk with the Lord along the path of hope (cf. *Spe Salvi*, 39). As

Pope John Paul II observed six years ago, "we must be confident that this time of trial will bring a purification of the entire Catholic community", leading to "a holier priesthood, a holier episcopate and a holier Church" (*Address to the Cardinals of the United States,* 23 April 2002, 4). There are many signs that, during the intervening period, such purification has indeed been taking place. Christ's abiding presence in the midst of our suffering is gradually transforming our darkness into light: all things are indeed being made new in Christ Jesus our hope.

At this stage a vital part of your task is to strengthen relationships with your clergy, especially in those cases where tension has arisen between priests and their bishops in the wake of the crisis. It is important that you continue to show them your concern, to support them, and to lead by example. In this way you will surely help them to encounter the living God, and point them towards the life-transforming hope of which the Gospel speaks. If you yourselves live in a manner closely configured to Christ, the Good Shepherd, who laid down his life for his sheep, you will inspire your brother priests to rededicate themselves to the service of their flocks with Christ-like generosity. Indeed a clearer focus upon the imitation of Christ in holiness of life is exactly what is needed in order for us to move forward. We need to rediscover the joy of living a Christ-centered life, cultivating the virtues, and immersing ourselves in prayer. When the faithful know that their pastor is a man who prays and who dedicates his life to serving them, they respond with warmth and affection which nourishes and sustains the life of the whole community.

Time spent in prayer is never wasted, however urgent the duties that press upon us from every side. Adoration of Christ our Lord in the Blessed Sacrament prolongs and intensifies the union with him that is established through the Eucharistic celebration (cf. *Sacramentum Caritatis,* 66).

Contemplation of the mysteries of the Rosary releases all their saving power and it conforms, unites and consecrates us to Jesus Christ (cf. *Rosarium Virginis Mariae,* 11, 15). Fidelity to the Liturgy of the Hours ensures that the whole of our day is sanctified and it continually reminds us of the need to remain focused on doing God's work, however many pressures and distractions may arise from the task at hand. Thus our devotion helps us to speak and act in persona Christi, to teach, govern and sanctify the faithful in the name of Jesus, to bring his reconciliation, his healing and his love to all his beloved brothers and sisters. This radical configuration to Christ, the Good Shepherd, lies at the heart of our pastoral ministry, and if we open ourselves through prayer to the power of the Spirit, he will give us the gifts we need to carry out our daunting task, so that we need never "be anxious how to speak or what to say" (*Matt* 10:19).

As I conclude my words to you this evening, I commend the Church in your country most particularly to the maternal care and intercession of Mary Immaculate, Patroness of the United States. May she who carried within her womb the hope of all the nations intercede for the people of this country, so that all may be made new in Jesus Christ her Son. My dear Brother Bishops, I assure each of you here present of my deep friendship and my participation in your pastoral concerns. To all of you, and to your clergy, religious and lay faithful, I cordially impart my Apostolic Blessing as a pledge of joy and peace in the Risen Lord.

RESPONSES OF HIS HOLINESS BENEDICT XVI TO THE QUESTIONS POSED BY THE BISHOPS

NATIONAL SHRINE OF THE IMMACULATE CONCEPTION IN WASHINGTON, D.C.
Wednesday, April 16, 2008

1. The Holy Father is asked to give his assessment of the challenge of increasing secularism in public life and relativism in intellectual life, and his advice on how to confront these challenges pastorally and evangelize more effectively.

I touched upon this theme briefly in my address. It strikes me as significant that here in America, unlike many places in Europe, the secular mentality has not been intrinsically opposed to religion. Within the context of the separation of Church and State, American society has always been marked by a fundamental respect for religion and its public role, and, if polls are to be believed, the American people are deeply religious. But it is not enough to count on this traditional religiosity and go about business as usual, even as its foundations are being slowly undermined. A serious commitment to evangelization cannot prescind from a profound

27

diagnosis of the real challenges the Gospel encounters in contemporary American culture.

Of course, what is essential is a correct understanding of the just autonomy of the secular order, an autonomy which cannot be divorced from God the Creator and his saving plan (cf. *Gaudium et Spes*, 36). Perhaps America's brand of secularism poses a particular problem: it allows for professing belief in God, and respects the public role of religion and the Churches, but at the same time it can subtly reduce religious belief to a lowest common denominator. Faith becomes a passive acceptance that certain things "out there" are true, but without practical relevance for everyday life. The result is a growing separation of faith from life: living "as if God did not exist". This is aggravated by an individualistic and eclectic approach to faith and religion: far from a Catholic approach to "thinking with the Church", each person believes he or she has a right to pick and choose, maintaining external social bonds but without an integral, interior conversion to the law of Christ. Consequently, rather than being transformed and renewed in mind, Christians are easily tempted to conform themselves to the spirit of this age (cf. *Rom* 12:3). We have seen this emerge in an acute way in the scandal given by Catholics who promote an alleged right to abortion.

On a deeper level, secularism challenges the Church to reaffirm and to pursue more actively her mission in and to the world. As the Council made clear, the lay faithful have a particular responsibility in this regard. What is needed, I am convinced, is a greater sense of the intrinsic relationship between the Gospel and the natural law on the one hand, and, on the other, the pursuit of authentic human good, as embodied in civil law and in personal moral decisions. In a society that rightly values personal liberty, the Church needs to promote at every level of her teaching—in catechesis, preaching, seminary and university instruction—an apologetics aimed at affirming the truth of Christian revelation, the harmony of faith and reason, and a sound understanding of freedom, seen in positive terms as a liberation both from the limitations of sin and *for* an authentic and fulfilling life. In a word, the Gospel has to be preached and taught as an integral way of life, offering an attractive and true answer, intellectually and practically, to real human problems. The "dictatorship of relativism", in the end, is nothing less than a threat to genuine human freedom, which only matures in generosity and fidelity to the truth.

Much more, of course, could be said on this subject: let me conclude, though, by saying that I believe that the Church in America, at this point in her history, is faced with the challenge of recapturing the Catholic vision of reality and presenting it, in an engaging and imaginative way, to a society which markets any number of recipes for human fulfillment. I think in particular of our need to speak to the hearts of young people, who, despite their constant exposure to messages contrary to the Gospel, continue to thirst for authenticity, goodness and truth. Much remains to be done, particularly on the level of preaching and catechesis in parishes and schools, if the new evangelization is to bear fruit for the renewal of ecclesial life in America.

2. The Holy Father is asked about "a certain quiet attrition" by which Catholics are abandoning the practice of the faith, sometimes by an explicit decision, but often by distancing themselves quietly and gradually from attendance at Mass and identification with the Church.

Certainly, much of this has to do with the passing away of a religious culture, sometimes disparagingly referred to as a "ghetto", which reinforced participation and identification with the Church. As I just mentioned, one of the great chal-

lenges facing the Church in this country is that of cultivating
a Catholic identity which is based not so much on externals
as on a way of thinking and acting grounded in the Gospel
and enriched by the Church's living tradition.

The issue clearly involves factors such as religious individualism and scandal. Let us go to the heart of the matter:
faith cannot survive unless it is nourished, unless it is
"formed by charity" (cf. *Gal* 5:6). Do people today find it
difficult to encounter God in our Churches? Has our preaching lost its salt? Might it be that many people have forgotten,
or never really learned, how to pray in and with the Church?

Here I am not speaking of people who leave the Church
in search of subjective religious "experiences"; this is a pastoral issue which must be addressed on its own terms. I think
we are speaking about people who have fallen by the wayside
without consciously having rejected their faith in Christ, but,
for whatever reason, have not drawn life from the liturgy, the
sacraments, preaching. Yet Christian faith, as we know, is
essentially ecclesial, and without a living bond to the community, the individual's faith will never grow to maturity.
Indeed, to return to the question I just discussed, the result
can be a quiet apostasy.

So let me make two brief observations on the problem
of "attrition", which I hope will stimulate further reflection.

First, as you know, it is becoming more and more difficult, in our Western societies, to speak in a meaningful way
of "salvation". Yet salvation—deliverance from the reality of
evil, and the gift of new life and freedom in Christ—is at the
heart of the Gospel. We need to discover, as I have suggested,
new and engaging ways of proclaiming this message and
awakening a thirst for the fulfillment which only Christ can
bring. It is in the Church's liturgy, and above all in the sacrament of the Eucharist, that these realities are most powerfully
expressed and lived in the life of believers; perhaps we still

have much to do in realizing the Council's vision of the liturgy as the exercise of the common priesthood and the impetus for a fruitful apostolate in the world.

Second, we need to acknowledge with concern the almost complete eclipse of an eschatological sense in many of our traditionally Christian societies. As you know, I have pointed to this problem in the Encyclical *Spe Salvi*. Suffice it to say that faith and hope are not limited to this world: as theological virtues, they unite us with the Lord and draw us toward the fulfillment not only of our personal destiny but also that of all creation. Faith and hope are the inspiration and basis of our efforts to prepare for the coming of the Kingdom of God. In Christianity, there can be no room for purely private religion: Christ is the Savior of the world, and, as members of his Body and sharers in his prophetic, priestly and royal *munera*, we cannot separate our love for him from our commitment to the building up of the Church and the extension of his Kingdom. To the extent that religion becomes a purely private affair, it loses its very soul.

Let me conclude by stating the obvious. The fields are still ripe for harvesting (cf. *John* 4:35); God continues to give the growth (cf. 1 *Cor* 3:6). We can and must believe, with the late Pope John Paul II, that God is preparing a new springtime for Christianity (cf. *Redemptoris Missio*, 86). What is needed above all, at this time in the history of the Church in America, is a renewal of that apostolic zeal which inspires her shepherds actively to seek out the lost, to bind up those who have been wounded, and to bring strength to those who are languishing (cf. *Ezek* 34:16). And this, as I have said, calls for new ways of thinking based on a sound diagnosis of today's challenges and a commitment to unity in the service of the Church's mission to the present generation.

3. The Holy Father is asked to comment on the decline in vocations despite the growing numbers of the Catholic population, and on the reasons for hope offered by the personal qualities and the thirst for holiness which characterize the candidates who do come forward.

Let us be quite frank: the ability to cultivate vocations to the priesthood and the religious life is a sure sign of the health of a local Church. There is no room for complacency in this regard. God continues to call young people; it is up to all of us to encourage a generous and free response to that call. On the other hand, none of us can take this grace for granted.

In the Gospel, Jesus tells us to pray that the Lord of the harvest will send workers. He even admits that the workers are few in comparison with the abundance of the harvest (cf. *Matt* 9:37–38). Strange to say, I often think that prayer—the *unum necessarium*—is the one aspect of vocations work which we tend to forget or to undervalue!

Nor am I speaking only of prayer *for vocations*. Prayer itself, born in Catholic families, nurtured by programs of Christian formation, strengthened by the grace of the sacraments, is the first means by which we come to know the Lord's will for our lives. To the extent that we teach young people to pray, and to pray well, we will be cooperating with God's call. Programs, plans and projects have their place; but the discernment of a vocation is above all the fruit of an intimate dialogue between the Lord and his disciples. Young people, if they know how to pray, can be trusted to know what to do with God's call.

It has been noted that there is a growing thirst for holiness in many young people today, and that, although fewer in number, those who come forward show great idealism and much promise. It is important to listen to them, to understand their experiences, and to encourage them to help their peers to see the need for committed priests and religious, as well as the beauty of a life of sacrificial service to the Lord and his Church. To my mind, much is demanded of vocation directors and formators: candidates today, as much as ever, need to be given a sound intellectual and human formation which will enable them not only to respond to the real questions and needs of their contemporaries, but also to mature in their own conversion and to persevere in life-long commitment to their vocation. As Bishops, you are conscious of the sacrifice demanded when you are asked to release one of your finest priests for seminary work. I urge you to respond with generosity, for the good of the whole Church.

Finally, I think you know from experience that most of your brother priests are happy in their vocation. What I said in my address about the importance of unity and cooperation within the presbyterate applies here too. There is a need for all of us to move beyond sterile divisions, disagreements and preconceptions, and to listen together to the voice of the Spirit who is guiding the Church into a future of hope. Each of us knows how important priestly fraternity has been in our lives. That fraternity is not only a precious possession, but also an immense resource for the renewal of the priesthood and the raising up of new vocations. I would close by encouraging you to foster opportunities for ever greater dialogue and fraternal encounter among your priests, and especially the younger priests. I am convinced that this will bear great fruit for their own enrichment, for the increase of their love for the priesthood and the Church, and for the effectiveness of their apostolate.

Dear Brother Bishops, with these few observations, I once more encourage all of you in your ministry to the faithful entrusted to your pastoral care, and I commend you to the loving intercession of Mary Immaculate, Mother of the Church.

PRESENTATION OF A CHALICE BY HIS HOLINESS BENEDICT XVI TO THE ARCHBISHOP OF NEW ORLEANS

NATIONAL SHRINE OF THE IMMACULATE CONCEPTION IN WASHINGTON, D.C.
Wednesday, April 16, 2008

Before leaving, I would like to pause to acknowledge the immense suffering endured by the people of God in the Archdiocese of New Orleans as a result of Hurricane Katrina, as well as their courage in the challenging work of rebuilding. I would like to present Archbishop Alfred Hughes with a chalice, which I hope will be accepted as a sign of my prayerful solidarity with the faithful of the Archdiocese, and my personal gratitude for the tireless devotion which he and Archbishops Philip Hannan and Francis Schulte showed toward the flock entrusted to their care.

HOMILY OF
HIS HOLINESS BENEDICT XVI
DURING MASS AT
NATIONALS PARK

NATIONALS PARK, WASHINGTON, D.C.
Thursday, April 17, 2008

DEAR BROTHERS AND SISTERS IN CHRIST,

"Peace be with you!" (*John* 20:19). With these, the first words of the Risen Lord to his disciples, I greet all of you in the joy of this Easter season. Before all else, I thank God for the blessing of being in your midst. I am particularly grateful to Archbishop Wuerl for his kind words of welcome.

Our Mass today brings the Church in the United States back to its roots in nearby Maryland, and commemorates the bicentennial of the first chapter of its remarkable growth—the division by my predecessor, Pope Pius VII, of the original Diocese of Baltimore and the establishment of the Dioceses of Boston, Bardstown (now Louisville), New York and Philadelphia. Two hundred years later, the Church in America can rightfully praise the accomplishment of past generations in bringing together widely differing immigrant groups within the unity of the Catholic faith and in a common commitment to the spread of the Gospel. At the same time, conscious of its rich diversity, the Catholic community in this country has come to appreciate ever more fully the importance of each individual and group offering its own particular gifts to the whole. The Church in the United States is now called to look to the future, firmly grounded in the faith passed on by previous generations, and ready to meet new challenges— challenges no less demanding than those faced by your forebears—with the hope born of God's love, poured into our hearts by the Holy Spirit (cf. *Rom* 5:5).

In the exercise of my ministry as the Successor of Peter, I have come to America to confirm you, my brothers and sisters, in the faith of the Apostles (cf. *Luke* 22:32). I have come to proclaim anew, as Peter proclaimed on the day of Pentecost, that Jesus Christ is Lord and Messiah, risen from the dead, seated in glory at the right hand of the Father, and established as judge of the living and the dead (cf. *Acts* 2:14ff.). I have come to repeat the Apostle's urgent call to conversion and the forgiveness of sins, and to implore from the Lord a new outpouring of the Holy Spirit upon the Church in this country. As we have heard throughout this Easter season, the Church was born of the Spirit's gift of repentance and faith in the risen Lord. In every age she is impelled by the same Spirit to bring to men and women of every race, language and people (cf. *Rev* 5:9) the good news of our reconciliation with God in Christ.

The readings of today's Mass invite us to consider the growth of the Church in America as one chapter in the greater story of the Church's expansion following the descent of the Holy Spirit at Pentecost. In those readings we see the inseparable link between the risen Lord, the gift of the Spirit for the forgiveness of sins, and the mystery of the Church. Christ established his Church on the foundation of the Apostles (cf. *Rev* 21:14) as a visible, structured community which is at the same time a spiritual communion, a mystical body enlivened by the Spirit's manifold gifts, and the sacrament of salvation for all humanity (cf. *Lumen Gentium,* 8). In every time and place, the Church is called to grow in unity through constant conversion to Christ, whose saving work is proclaimed by the Successors of the Apostles and celebrated in the sacraments. This unity, in turn, gives rise to an unceasing missionary outreach, as the Spirit spurs believers to proclaim "the great works of God" and to invite all people to enter the community of those saved by the blood of Christ and granted new life in his Spirit.

I pray, then, that this significant anniversary in the life of the Church in the United States, and the presence of the Successor of Peter in your midst, will be an occasion for all Catholics to reaffirm their unity in the apostolic faith, to offer their contemporaries a convincing account of the hope which inspires them (cf. 1 *Pet* 3:15), and to be renewed in missionary zeal for the extension of God's Kingdom.

The world needs this witness! Who can deny that the present moment is a crossroads, not only for the Church in America but also for society as a whole? It is a time of great promise, as we see the human family in many ways drawing closer together and becoming ever more interdependent. Yet at the same time we see clear signs of a disturbing breakdown in the very foundations of society: signs of alienation, anger and polarization on the part of many of our contemporaries; increased violence; a weakening of the moral sense; a coarsening of social relations; and a growing forgetfulness of Christ and God. The Church, too, sees signs of immense promise in her many strong parishes and vital movements, in the enthusiasm for the faith shown by so many young people, in the number of those who each year embrace the Catholic faith, and in a greater interest in prayer and catechesis. At the same time she senses, often painfully, the presence of division and polarization in her midst, as well as the troubling realization that many of the baptized, rather than acting as a spiritual leaven in the world, are inclined to embrace attitudes contrary to the truth of the Gospel.

"Lord, send out your Spirit, and renew the face of the earth!" (cf. *Ps* 104:30). The words of today's Responsorial Psalm are a prayer which rises up from the heart of the Church in every time and place. They remind us that the Holy Spirit has been poured out as the first fruits of a new creation, "new heavens and a new earth" (cf. 2 *Pet* 3:13; *Rev* 21:1), in which God's peace will reign and the human family will be reconciled in justice and love. We have heard Saint Paul tell us that all creation is even now "groaning" in expectation of that true freedom which is God's gift to his children (*Rom* 8:21–22), a freedom which enables us to live in conformity to his will. Today let us pray fervently that the Church in America will be renewed in that same Spirit, and sustained in her mission of proclaiming the Gospel to a world that longs for genuine freedom (cf. *John* 8:32), authentic happiness, and the fulfillment of its deepest aspirations!

Here I wish to offer a special word of gratitude and encouragement to all those who have taken up the challenge of the Second Vatican Council, so often reiterated by Pope John Paul II, and committed their lives to the new evangelization. I thank my brother Bishops, priests and deacons, men and women religious, parents, teachers and catechists. The fidelity and courage with which the Church in this country will respond to the challenges raised by an increasingly secular and materialistic culture will depend in large part upon your own fidelity in handing on the treasure of our Catholic faith. Young people need to be helped to discern the path that leads to true freedom: the path of a sincere and generous imitation of Christ, the path of commitment to justice and peace. Much progress has been made in developing solid programs of catechesis, yet so much more remains to be done in forming the hearts and minds of the young in knowledge and love of the Lord. The challenges confronting us require a comprehensive and sound instruction in the truths of the faith. But they also call for cultivating a mindset, an intellectual "culture", which is genuinely Catholic, confident in the profound harmony of faith and reason, and prepared to bring the richness of faith's vision to bear on the urgent issues which affect the future of American society.

Dear friends, my visit to the United States is meant to be a witness to "Christ our Hope". Americans have always been a people of hope: your ancestors came to this country with the expectation of finding new freedom and opportunity, while the vastness of the unexplored wilderness inspired in them the hope of being able to start completely anew, building a new nation on new foundations. To be sure, this promise was not experienced by all the inhabitants of this land; one thinks of the injustices endured by the native American peoples and by those brought here forcibly from Africa as slaves. Yet hope, hope for the future, is very much a part of the American character. And the Christian virtue of hope— the hope poured into our hearts by the Holy Spirit, the hope which supernaturally purifies and corrects our aspirations by focusing them on the Lord and his saving plan—that hope has also marked, and continues to mark, the life of the Catholic community in this country.

It is in the context of this hope born of God's love and fidelity that I acknowledge the pain which the Church in America has experienced as a result of the sexual abuse of minors. No words of mine could describe the pain and harm inflicted by such abuse. It is important that those who have suffered be given loving pastoral attention. Nor can I adequately describe the damage that has occurred within the community of the Church. Great efforts have already been made to deal honestly and fairly with this tragic situation, and to ensure that children—whom our Lord loves so deeply (cf. *Mark* 10:14), and who are our greatest treasure—can grow up in a safe environment. These efforts to protect children must continue. Yesterday I spoke with your Bishops about this. Today I encourage each of you to do what you can to foster healing and reconciliation, and to assist those who have been hurt. Also, I ask you to love your priests, and to affirm them in the excellent work that they do. And above all, pray that the Holy Spirit will pour out his gifts upon the Church, the gifts that lead to conversion, forgiveness and growth in holiness.

Saint Paul speaks, as we heard in the second reading, of a kind of prayer which arises from the depths of our hearts in sighs too deep for words, in "groanings" (*Rom* 8:26) inspired by the Spirit. This is a prayer which yearns, in the midst of chastisement, for the fulfillment of God's promises. It is a prayer of unfailing hope, but also one of patient endurance and, often, accompanied by suffering for the truth. Through this prayer, we share in the mystery of Christ's own weakness and suffering, while trusting firmly in the victory of his Cross. With this prayer, may the Church in America embrace ever more fully the way of conversion and fidelity to the demands of the Gospel. And may all Catholics experience the consolation of hope, and the Spirit's gifts of joy and strength.

In today's Gospel, the risen Lord bestows the gift of the Holy Spirit upon the Apostles and grants them the authority to forgive sins. Through the surpassing power of Christ's grace, entrusted to frail human ministers, the Church is constantly reborn and each of us is given the hope of a new beginning. Let us trust in the Spirit's power to inspire conversion, to heal every wound, to overcome every division, and to inspire new life and freedom. How much we need these gifts! And how close at hand they are, particularly in the sacrament of Penance! The liberating power of this sacrament, in which our honest confession of sin is met by God's merciful word of pardon and peace, needs to be rediscovered and reappropriated by every Catholic. To a great extent, the renewal of the Church in America and throughout the world depends on the renewal of the practice of Penance and the growth in holiness which that sacrament both inspires and accomplishes.

"In hope we were saved!" (*Rom* 8:24)." As the Church in the United States gives thanks for the blessings of the past two hundred years, I invite you, your families, and every parish and religious community, to trust in the power of grace to create a future of promise for God's people in this country. I ask you, in the Lord Jesus, to set aside all division and to work with joy to prepare a way for him, in fidelity to his word and in constant conversion to his will. Above all, I urge you to continue to be a leaven of evangelical hope in American society, striving to bring the light and truth of the Gospel to the task of building an ever more just and free world for generations yet to come.

Those who have hope must live different lives! (cf. *Spe Salvi*, 2). By your prayers, by the witness of your faith, by the fruitfulness of your charity, may you point the way towards that vast horizon of hope which God is even now opening up to his Church, and indeed to all humanity: the vision of a world reconciled and renewed in Christ Jesus, our Savior. To him be all honor and glory, now and forever. Amen!

QUERIDOS HERMANOS Y HERMANAS DE LENGUA ESPAÑOLA:

Deseo saludarles con las mismas palabras que Cristo Resucitado dirigió a los apóstoles: "Paz a ustedes" (*John* 20:19). Que la alegría de saber que el Señor ha triunfado sobre la muerte y el pecado les ayude a ser, allá donde se encuentren, testigos de su amor y sembradores de la esperanza que Él vino a traernos y que jamás defrauda.

No se dejen vencer por el pesimismo, la inercia o los problemas. Antes bien, fieles a los compromisos que adquirieron en su bautismo, profundicen cada día en el conocimiento de Cristo y permitan que su corazón quede conquistado por su amor y por su perdón.

La Iglesia en los Estados Unidos, acogiendo en su seno a tantos de sus hijos emigrantes, ha ido creciendo gracias también a la vitalidad del testimonio de fe de los fieles de lengua española. Por eso, el Señor les llama a seguir contribuyendo al futuro de la Iglesia en este País y a la difusión del Evangelio. Sólo si están unidos a Cristo y entre ustedes, su testimonio evangelizador será creíble y florecerá en copiosos frutos de paz y reconciliación en medio de un mundo muchas veces marcado por divisiones y enfrentamientos.

La Iglesia espera mucho de ustedes. No la defrauden en su donación generosa. "Lo que han recibido gratis, denlo gratis" (*Matt* 10:8). Amen!

ADDRESS OF HIS HOLINESS BENEDICT XVI TO CATHOLIC EDUCATORS

CONFERENCE HALL OF THE CATHOLIC UNIVERSITY OF AMERICA IN WASHINGTON, D.C.
Thursday, April 17, 2008

YOUR EMINENCES,

DEAR BROTHER BISHOPS,

DISTINGUISHED PROFESSORS, TEACHERS AND EDUCATORS,

"How beautiful are the footsteps of those who bring good news" (*Rom* 10:15–17). With these words of Isaiah quoted by Saint Paul, I warmly greet each of you—bearers of wisdom—and through you the staff, students and families of the many and varied institutions of learning that you represent. It is my great pleasure to meet you and to share with you some thoughts regarding the nature and identity of Catholic education today. I especially wish to thank Father David O'Connell, President and Rector of the Catholic University of America. Your kind words of welcome are much appreciated.

43

Please extend my heartfelt gratitude to the entire community—faculty, staff and students—of this University.

Education is integral to the mission of the Church to proclaim the Good News. First and foremost every Catholic educational institution is a place to encounter the living God who in Jesus Christ reveals his transforming love and truth (cf. *Spe Salvi*, 4). This relationship elicits a desire to grow in the knowledge and understanding of Christ and his teaching. In this way those who meet him are drawn by the very power of the Gospel to lead a new life characterized by all that is beautiful, good, and true; a life of Christian witness nurtured and strengthened within the community of our Lord's disciples, the Church.

The dynamic between personal encounter, knowledge and Christian witness is integral to the *diakonia* of truth which the Church exercises in the midst of humanity. God's revelation offers every generation the opportunity to discover the ultimate truth about its own life and the goal of history. This task is never easy; it involves the entire Christian community and motivates each generation of Christian educators to ensure that the power of God's truth permeates every dimension of the institutions they serve. In this way, Christ's Good News is set to work, guiding both teacher and student towards the objective truth which, in transcending the particular and the subjective, points to the universal and absolute that enables us to proclaim with confidence the hope which does not disappoint (cf. *Rom* 5:5). Set against personal struggles, moral confusion and fragmentation of knowledge, the noble goals of scholarship and education, founded on the unity of truth and in service of the person and the community, become an especially powerful instrument of hope.

Dear friends, the history of this nation includes many examples of the Church's commitment in this regard. The Catholic community here has in fact made education one of its highest priorities. This undertaking has not come without great sacrifice. Towering figures, like Saint Elizabeth Ann Seton and other founders and foundresses, with great tenacity and foresight, laid the foundations of what is today a remarkable network of parochial schools contributing to the spiritual well-being of the Church and the nation. Some, like Saint Katharine Drexel, devoted their lives to educating those whom others had neglected—in her case, African Americans and Native Americans. Countless dedicated Religious Sisters, Brothers, and Priests together with selfless parents have, through Catholic schools, helped generations of immigrants to rise from poverty and take their place in mainstream society.

This sacrifice continues today. It is an outstanding apostolate of hope, seeking to address the material, intellectual and spiritual needs of over three million children and students. It also provides a highly commendable opportunity for the entire Catholic community to contribute generously to the financial needs of our institutions. Their long-term sustainability must be assured. Indeed, everything possible must be done, in cooperation with the wider community, to ensure that they are accessible to people of all social and economic strata. No child should be denied his or her right to an education in faith, which in turn nurtures the soul of a nation.

Some today question the Church's involvement in education, wondering whether her resources might be better placed elsewhere. Certainly in a nation such as this, the State provides ample opportunities for education and attracts committed and generous men and women to this honorable profession. It is timely, then, to reflect on what is particular to our Catholic institutions. How do they contribute to the good of society through the Church's primary mission of evangelization?

All the Church's activities stem from her awareness that she is the bearer of a message which has its origin in God himself: in his goodness and wisdom, God chose to reveal himself and to make known the hidden purpose of his will (cf. *Eph* 1:9; *Dei Verbum*, 2). God's desire to make himself known, and the innate desire of all human beings to know the truth, provide the context for human inquiry into the meaning of life. This unique encounter is sustained within our Christian community: the one who seeks the truth becomes the one who lives by faith (cf. *Fides et Ratio*, 31). It can be described as a move from "I" to "we", leading the individual to be numbered among God's people.

This same dynamic of communal identity—to whom do I belong?—vivifies the ethos of our Catholic institutions. A university or school's Catholic identity is not simply a question of the number of Catholic students. It is a question of conviction—do we really believe that only in the mystery of the Word made flesh does the mystery of man truly become clear (cf. *Gaudium et Spes*, 22)? Are we ready to commit our entire self—intellect and will, mind and heart—to God? Do we accept the truth Christ reveals? Is the faith tangible in our universities and schools? Is it given fervent expression liturgically, sacramentally, through prayer, acts of charity, a concern for justice, and respect for God's creation? Only in this way do we really bear witness to the meaning of who we are and what we uphold.

From this perspective one can recognize that the contemporary "crisis of truth" is rooted in a "crisis of faith". Only through faith can we freely give our assent to God's testimony and acknowledge him as the transcendent guarantor of the truth he reveals. Again, we see why fostering personal intimacy with Jesus Christ and communal witness to his loving truth is indispensable in Catholic institutions of learning. Yet we all know, and observe with concern, the difficulty or reluctance many people have today in entrusting themselves to God. It is a complex phenomenon and one which I ponder continually. While we have sought diligently to engage the intellect of our young, perhaps we have neglected the will. Subsequently we observe, with distress, the notion of freedom being distorted. Freedom is not an opting out. It is an opting in—a participation in Being itself. Hence authentic freedom can never be attained by turning away from God. Such a choice would ultimately disregard the very truth we need in order to understand ourselves. A particular responsibility therefore for each of you, and your colleagues, is to evoke among the young the desire for the act of faith, encouraging them to commit themselves to the ecclesial life that follows from this belief. It is here that freedom reaches the certainty of truth. In choosing to live by that truth, we embrace the fullness of the life of faith which is given to us in the Church.

Clearly, then, Catholic identity is not dependent upon statistics. Neither can it be equated simply with orthodoxy of course content. It demands and inspires much more: namely that each and every aspect of your learning communities reverberates within the ecclesial life of faith. Only in faith can truth become incarnate and reason truly human, capable of directing the will along the path of freedom (cf. *Spe Salvi,* 23). In this way our institutions make a vital contribution to the mission of the Church and truly serve society. They become places in which God's active presence in human affairs is recognized and in which every young person discovers the joy of entering into Christ's "being for others" (cf. *ibid.,* 28).

The Church's primary mission of evangelization, in which educational institutions play a crucial role, is consonant with a nation's fundamental aspiration to develop a society truly worthy of the human person's dignity. At times, however, the value of the Church's contribution to the public forum is questioned. It is important therefore to recall that the truths of faith and of reason never contradict one another (cf. First Vatican Ecumenical Council, Dogmatic Constitution on the Catholic Faith *Dei Filius,* IV: DS 3017; St. Augustine, *Contra Academicos,* III, 20, 43). The Church's mission, in fact, involves her in humanity's struggle to arrive at truth. In articulating revealed truth she serves all members of society by purifying reason, ensuring that it remains open to the consideration of ultimate truths. Drawing upon divine wisdom, she sheds light on the foundation of human morality and ethics, and reminds all groups in society that it is not praxis that creates truth but truth that should serve as the basis of praxis. Far from undermining the tolerance of legitimate diversity, such a contribution illuminates the very truth which makes consensus attainable, and helps to keep public debate rational, honest and accountable. Similarly the Church never tires of upholding the essential moral categories of right and wrong, without which hope could only wither, giving way to cold pragmatic calculations of utility which render the person little more than a pawn on some ideological chess-board.

With regard to the educational forum, the *diakonia* of truth takes on a heightened significance in societies where secularist ideology drives a wedge between truth and faith. This division has led to a tendency to equate truth with knowledge and to adopt a positivistic mentality which, in rejecting metaphysics, denies the foundations of faith and rejects the need for a moral vision. Truth means more than knowledge: knowing the truth leads us to discover the good. Truth speaks to the individual in his or her entirety, inviting us to respond with our whole being. This optimistic vision is found in our Christian faith because such faith has been granted the vision of the *Logos,* God's creative Reason, which in the Incarnation, is revealed as Goodness itself. Far from being just a communication of factual data—"informative"—the loving truth of the Gospel is creative and life-changing—"performative" (cf. *Spe Salvi* 2). With confidence, Christian educators can liberate the young from the limits of positivism and awaken receptivity to the truth, to God and his goodness. In this way you will also help to form their conscience which, enriched by faith, opens a sure path to inner peace and to respect for others.

It comes as no surprise, then, that not just our own ecclesial communities but society in general has high expectations of Catholic educators. This places upon you a responsibility and offers an opportunity. More and more people—parents in particular—recognize the need for excellence in the human formation of their children. As *Mater et Magistra*, the Church shares their concern. When nothing beyond the individual is recognized as definitive, the ultimate criterion of judgment becomes the self and the satisfaction of the individual's immediate wishes. The objectivity and perspective, which can only come through a recognition of the essential transcendent dimension of the human person, can be lost. Within such a relativistic horizon the goals of education are inevitably curtailed. Slowly, a lowering of standards occurs. We observe today a timidity in the face of the category of the good and an aimless pursuit of novelty parading as the realization of freedom. We witness an assumption that every experience is of equal worth and a reluctance to admit imperfection and mistakes. And particularly disturbing, is the reduction of the precious and delicate area of education in sexuality to management of 'risk', bereft of any reference to the beauty of conjugal love.

How might Christian educators respond? These harmful developments point to the particular urgency of what we might call "intellectual charity". This aspect of charity calls the educator to recognize that the profound responsibility to lead the young to truth is nothing less than an act of love. Indeed, the dignity of education lies in fostering the true perfection and happiness of those to be educated. In practice "intellectual charity" upholds the essential unity of knowledge against the fragmentation which ensues when reason is detached from the pursuit of truth. It guides the young towards the deep satisfaction of exercising freedom in relation to truth, and it strives to articulate the relationship between faith and all aspects of family and civic life. Once their passion for the fullness and unity of truth has been awakened, young people will surely relish the discovery that the question of what they can know opens up the vast adventure of what they ought to do. Here they will experience "in what" and "in whom" it is possible to hope, and be inspired to contribute to society in a way that engenders hope in others.

Dear friends, I wish to conclude by focusing our attention specifically on the paramount importance of your own professionalism and witness within our Catholic universities and schools. First, let me thank you for your dedication and generosity. I know from my own days as a professor, and I have heard from your Bishops and officials of the Congregation for Catholic Education, that the reputation of Catholic institutes of learning in this country is largely due to yourselves and your predecessors. Your selfless contributions—from outstanding research to the dedication of those working in inner-city schools—serve both your country and the Church. For this I express my profound gratitude.

In regard to faculty members at Catholic colleges universities, I wish to reaffirm the great value of academic freedom. In virtue of this freedom you are called to search for the truth wherever careful analysis of evidence leads you. Yet it is also the case that any appeal to the principle of academic freedom in order to justify positions that contradict the faith and the teaching of the Church would obstruct or even betray the university's identity and mission; a mission at the heart of the Church's *munus docendi* and not somehow autonomous or independent of it.

Teachers and administrators, whether in universities or schools, have the duty and privilege to ensure that students receive instruction in Catholic doctrine and practice. This requires that public witness to the way of Christ, as found in the Gospel and upheld by the Church's Magisterium, shapes all aspects of an institution's life, both inside and outside the classroom. Divergence from this vision weakens Catholic identity and, far from advancing freedom, inevitably leads to confusion, whether moral, intellectual or spiritual.

I wish also to express a particular word of encouragement to both lay and Religious teachers of catechesis who strive to ensure that young people become daily more appreciative of the gift of faith. Religious education is a challenging apostolate, yet there are many signs of a desire among young people to learn about the faith and practice it with vigor. If this awakening is to grow, teachers require a clear and precise understanding of the specific nature and role of Catholic education. They must also be ready to lead the commitment made by the entire school community to assist our young people, and their families, to experience the harmony between faith, life and culture.

Here I wish to make a special appeal to Religious Brothers, Sisters and Priests: do not abandon the school apostolate; indeed, renew your commitment to schools especially those in poorer areas. In places where there are many hollow promises which lure young people away from the path of truth and genuine freedom, the consecrated person's witness to the evangelical counsels is an irreplaceable gift. I encourage the Religious present to bring renewed enthusiasm to the promotion of vocations. Know that your witness to the ideal of consecration and mission among the young is a source of great inspiration in faith for them and their families.

To all of you I say: bear witness to hope. Nourish your witness with prayer. Account for the hope that characterizes your lives (cf. *1 Pet* 3:15) by living the truth which you propose to your students. Help them to know and love the One you have encountered, whose truth and goodness you have experienced with joy. With Saint Augustine, let us say: "we who speak and you who listen acknowledge ourselves as fellow disciples of a single teacher" (*Sermons*, 23:2). With these sentiments of communion, I gladly impart to you, your colleagues and students, and to your families, my Apostolic Blessing.

ADDRESS OF HIS HOLINESS BENEDICT XVI TO REPRESENTATIVES OF OTHER RELIGIONS

"ROTUNDA" HALL OF THE POPE JOHN PAUL II CULTURAL CENTER OF WASHINGTON, D.C.
Thursday, April 17, 2008

MY DEAR FRIENDS,

I am pleased to have this occasion to meet with you today. I thank Bishop Sklba for his words of welcome, and I cordially greet all those in attendance representing various religions in the United States of America. Several of you kindly accepted the invitation to compose the reflections contained in today's program. For your thoughtful words on how each of your traditions bears witness to peace, I am particularly grateful. Thank you all.

This country has a long history of cooperation between different religions in many spheres of public life. Interreligious prayer services during the national feast of Thanksgiving, joint initiatives in charitable activities, a shared voice on important public issues: these are some ways in which members of different religions come together to enhance mutual understanding and promote the common good. I encourage all religious groups in America to persevere in their collaboration and thus enrich public life with the spiritual values that motivate your action in the world.

The place where we are now gathered was founded specifically for promoting this type of collaboration. Indeed, the Pope John Paul II Cultural Center seeks to offer a Christian voice to the "human search for meaning and purpose in life" in a world of "varied religious, ethnic and cultural communities" *(Mission Statement)*. This institution reminds us of this nation's conviction that all people should be free to pursue happiness in a way consonant with their nature as creatures endowed with reason and free will.

Americans have always valued the ability to worship freely and in accordance with their conscience. Alexis de Tocqueville, the French historian and observer of American affairs, was fascinated with this aspect of the nation. He remarked that this is a country in which religion and freedom are "intimately linked" in contributing to a stable democracy that fosters social virtues and participation in the communal life of all its citizens. In urban areas, it is common for individuals from different cultural backgrounds and religions to engage with one another daily in commercial, social and educational settings. Today, in classrooms throughout the country, young Christians, Jews, Muslims, Hindus, Buddhists, and indeed children of all religions sit side-by-side, learning with one another and from one another. This diversity gives rise to new challenges that spark a deeper reflection on the core principles of a democratic society. May others take heart from your experience, realizing that a united society can indeed arise from a plurality of peoples—*"E pluribus unum"*: "out of many, one"—provided that all recognize religious liberty as a basic civil right (cf. *Dignitatis Humanae, 2*).

The task of upholding religious freedom is never completed. New situations and challenges invite citizens and leaders to reflect on how their decisions respect this basic human right. Protecting religious freedom within the rule of law does not guarantee that peoples—particularly minorities—will be spared from unjust forms of discrimination and prejudice. This requires constant effort on the part of all members of society to ensure that citizens are afforded the opportunity to worship peaceably and to pass on their religious heritage to their children.

The transmission of religious traditions to succeeding generations not only helps to preserve a heritage; it also sustains and nourishes the surrounding culture in the present day. The same holds true for dialogue between religions; both the participants and society are enriched. As we grow in understanding of one another, we see that we share an esteem for ethical values, discernable to human reason, which are revered by all peoples of goodwill. The world begs for a common witness to these values. I therefore invite all religious people to view dialogue not only as a means of enhancing mutual understanding, but also as a way of serving society at large. By bearing witness to those moral truths which they hold in common with all men and women of goodwill, religious groups will exert a positive influence on the wider culture, and inspire neighbors, co-workers and fellow citizens to join in the task of strengthening the ties of solidarity. In the words of President Franklin Delano Roosevelt: "no greater thing could come to our land today than a revival of the spirit of faith".

A concrete example of the contribution religious communities make to civil society is faith-based schools. These institutions enrich children both intellectually and spiritually. Led by their teachers to discover the divinely bestowed dignity of each human being, young people learn to respect the beliefs and practices of others, thus enhancing a nation's civic life.

What an enormous responsibility religious leaders have: to imbue society with a profound awe and respect for human life and freedom; to ensure that human dignity is recognized and cherished; to facilitate peace and justice; to teach children what is right, good and reasonable!

There is a further point I wish to touch upon here. I have noticed a growing interest among governments to sponsor programs intended to promote interreligious and intercultural dialogue. These are praiseworthy initiatives. At the same time, religious freedom, interreligious dialogue and faith-based education aim at something more than a consensus regarding ways to implement practical strategies for advancing peace. The broader purpose of dialogue is to discover the truth. What is the origin and destiny of mankind? What are good and evil? What awaits us at the end of our earthly existence? Only by addressing these deeper questions can we build a solid basis for the peace and security of the human family, for "wherever and whenever men and women are enlightened by the splendor of truth, they naturally set out on the path of peace" (*Message for the 2006 World Day of Peace*, 3).

We are living in an age when these questions are too often marginalized. Yet they can never be erased from the human heart. Throughout history, men and women have striven to articulate their restlessness with this passing world. In the Judeo-Christian tradition, the Psalms are full of such expressions: "My spirit is overwhelmed within me" (*Ps* 143:4; cf. *Pss* 6:6, 31:10, 32:3, 38:8, 77:3); "why are you cast down, my soul, why groan within me?" (*Ps* 42:5). The response is always one of faith: "Hope in God, I will praise him still; my Savior and my God" (*Ps* 42:5, 11; cf. *Pss* 43:5, 62:5). Spiritual leaders have a special duty, and we might say competence, to place the deeper questions at the forefront of human consciousness, to reawaken mankind to the mystery of human existence, and to make space in a frenetic world for reflection and prayer.

Confronted with these deeper questions concerning the origin and destiny of mankind, Christianity proposes Jesus of Nazareth. He, we believe, is the eternal Logos who became flesh in order to reconcile man to God and reveal the underlying reason of all things. It is he whom we bring to the forum of interreligious dialogue. The ardent desire to follow in his footsteps spurs Christians to open their minds and hearts in dialogue (cf. *Luke* 10:25–37; *John* 4:7–26).

Dear friends, in our attempt to discover points of commonality, perhaps we have shied away from the responsibility to discuss our differences with calmness and clarity. While always uniting our hearts and minds in the call for peace, we must also listen attentively to the voice of truth. In this way, our dialogue will not stop at identifying a common set of values, but go on to probe their ultimate foundation. We have no reason to fear, for the truth unveils for us the essential relationship between the world and God. We are able to perceive that peace is a "heavenly gift" that calls us to conform human history to the divine order. Herein lies the "truth of peace" *(Message for the 2006 World Day of Peace)*.

As we have seen then, the higher goal of interreligious dialogue requires a clear exposition of our respective religious tenets. In this regard, colleges, universities and study centers are important forums for a candid exchange of religious ideas. The Holy See, for its part, seeks to carry forward this important work through the Pontifical Council for Interreligious Dialogue, the Pontifical Institute for Arabic and Islamic Studies, and various Pontifical Universities.

Dear friends, let our sincere dialogue and cooperation inspire all people to ponder the deeper questions of their origin and destiny. May the followers of all religions stand together in defending and promoting life and religious freedom everywhere. By giving ourselves generously to this sacred task—through dialogue and countless small acts of love, understanding and compassion—we can be instruments of peace for the whole human family.

GREETINGS OF
HIS HOLINESS BENEDICT XVI
TO REPRESENTATIVES OF
THE JEWISH COMMUNITY

"ROTUNDA" HALL OF THE POPE JOHN PAUL II CULTURAL CENTER OF WASHINGTON, D.C.
Thursday, April 17, 2008

MY DEAR FRIENDS,

I extend special greetings of peace to the Jewish community in the United States and throughout the world as you prepare to celebrate the annual feast of *Pesah*. My visit to this country has coincided with this feast, allowing me to meet with you personally and to assure you of my prayers as you recall the signs and wonders God performed in liberating his chosen people. Motivated by our common spiritual heritage, I am pleased to entrust to you this message as a testimony to our hope centered on the Almighty and his mercy.

MESSAGE OF
HIS HOLINESS BENEDICT XVI
TO THE JEWISH COMMUNITY
ON THE FEAST OF *PESAH*

"ROTUNDA" HALL OF THE POPE JOHN
PAUL II CULTURAL CENTER OF
WASHINGTON, D.C.
Thursday, April 17, 2008

**TO THE JEWISH COMMUNITY ON THE
FEAST OF *PESAH*:**

My visit to the United States offers me the occasion to extend a warm and heartfelt greeting to my Jewish brothers and sisters in this country and throughout the world. A greeting that is all the more spiritually intense because the great feast of *Pesah* is approaching. "This day shall be for you a memorial day, and you shall keep it as a feast to the Lord; throughout your generations you shall observe it as an ordinance for ever" (*Exod* 12:14). While the Christian celebration of Easter differs in many ways from your celebration of *Pesah*, we understand and experience it in continuation with the biblical narrative of the mighty works which the Lord accomplished for his people.

At this time of your most solemn celebration, I feel particularly close, precisely because of what *Nostra Aetate* calls Christians to remember always: that the Church "received the revelation of the Old Testament through the people with whom God in His inexpressible mercy concluded the Ancient Covenant. Nor can she forget that she draws sustenance from the root of that well-cultivated olive tree onto which have been grafted the wild shoots, the Gentiles" (*Nostra Aetate*, 4). In addressing myself to you I wish to re-affirm the Second Vatican Council's teaching on Catholic-Jewish relations and reiterate the Church's commitment to the dialogue that in the past forty years has fundamentally changed our relationship for the better.

Because of that growth in trust and friendship, Christians and Jews can rejoice together in the deep spiritual ethos of the Passover, a memorial *(zikkarôn)* of freedom and redemption. Each year, when we listen to the Passover story we return to that blessed night of liberation. This holy time of the year should be a call to both our communities to pursue justice, mercy, solidarity with the stranger in the land, with the widow and orphan, as Moses commanded: "But you shall remember that you were a slave in Egypt and the Lord your God redeemed you from there; therefore I command you to do this" (*Deut* 24:18).

At the Passover *Sèder* you recall the holy patriarchs Abraham, Isaac and Jacob, and the holy women of Israel, Sarah, Rebecca, Rachael and Leah, the beginning of the long line of sons and daughters of the Covenant. With the passing of time the Covenant assumes an ever more universal value, as the promise made to Abraham takes form: "I will bless you and make your name great, so that you will be a blessing... All the communities of the earth shall find blessing in you" (*Gen* 12:2–3). Indeed, according to the prophet Isaiah, the hope of redemption extends to the whole of humanity: "Many peoples will come and say: 'Come, let us go up to the mountain of the Lord, to the house of the God of Jacob; that he may teach us his ways and that we may walk in his paths'" (*Isa* 2:3). Within this eschatological horizon is offered a real prospect of universal brotherhood on the path of justice and peace, preparing the way of the Lord (cf. *Isa* 62:10).

Christians and Jews share this hope; we are in fact, as the prophets say, "prisoners of hope" (*Zech* 9:12). This bond permits us Christians to celebrate alongside you, though in our own way, the Passover of Christ's death and resurrection, which we see as inseparable from your own, for Jesus himself said: "salvation is from the Jews" (*John* 4:22). Our Easter and your *Pesah,* while distinct and different, unite us in our common hope centered on God and his mercy. They urge us to cooperate with each other and with all men and women of goodwill to make this a better world for all as we await the fulfillment of God's promises.

With respect and friendship, I therefore ask the Jewish community to accept my *Pesah* greeting in a spirit of openness to the real possibilities of cooperation which we see before us as we contemplate the urgent needs of our world, and as we look with compassion upon the sufferings of millions of our brothers and sisters everywhere. Naturally, our shared hope for peace in the world embraces the Middle East and the Holy Land in particular. May the memory of God's mercies, which Jews and Christians celebrate at this festive time, inspire all those responsible for the future of that region—where the events surrounding God's revelation actually took place—to new efforts, and especially to new attitudes and a new purification of hearts!

In my heart I repeat with you the psalm of the paschal *Hallel* (*Psalm* 118:1–4), invoking abundant divine blessings upon you:

"O give thanks to the Lord, for he is good; his steadfast
    love endures forever.
Let Israel say, 'His steadfast love endures forever.'…
Let those who fear the Lord say, 'His steadfast love
    endures forever'."

BENEDICTUS PP. XVI

From the Vatican, 14 April 2008

ADDRESS OF
HIS HOLINESS BENEDICT XVI
TO THE GENERAL ASSEMBLY
OF THE UNITED NATIONS

NEW YORK
Friday, April 18, 2008

MR. PRESIDENT,

LADIES AND GENTLEMEN,

As I begin my address to this Assembly, I would like first of all to express to you, Mr. President, my sincere gratitude for your kind words. My thanks go also to the Secretary-General, Mr. Ban Ki-moon, for inviting me to visit the head-quarters of this Organization and for the welcome that he has extended to me. I greet the Ambassadors and Diplomats from the Member States, and all those present. Through you, I greet the peoples who are represented here. They look to this institution to carry forward the founding inspiration to establish a "centre for harmonizing the actions of nations in the attainment of these common ends" of peace and develop-ment (cf. *Charter of the United Nations*, article 1.2–1.4). As Pope John Paul II expressed it in 1995, the Organization should be "a moral centre where all the nations of the world feel at home and develop a shared awareness of being, as it were, a 'family of nations'" (*Address to the General Assembly of the United Nations on the 50th Anniversary of its Foundation,* 5 October 1995, 14).

Through the United Nations, States have established universal objectives which, even if they do not coincide with the total common good of the human family, undoubtedly represent a fundamental part of that good. The founding principles of the Organization—the desire for peace, the quest for justice, respect for the dignity of the person, humanitarian cooperation and assistance—express the just aspirations of the human spirit, and constitute the ideals which should underpin international relations. As my predecessors Paul VI and John Paul II have observed from this very podium, all this is something that the Catholic Church and the Holy See follow attentively and with interest, seeing in your activity an example of how issues and conflicts concerning the world community can be subject to common regulation. The United Nations embodies the aspiration for a "greater degree of international ordering" (John Paul II, *Sollicitudo Rei Socialis,* 43), inspired and governed by the principle of subsidiarity, and therefore capable of responding to the demands of the human family through binding international rules and through structures capable of harmonizing the day-to-day unfolding of the lives of peoples. This is all the more necessary at a time when we experience the obvious paradox of a multilateral consensus that continues to be in crisis because it is still subordinated to the decisions of a few, whereas the world's problems call for interventions in the form of collective action by the international community.

Indeed, questions of security, development goals, reduction of local and global inequalities, protection of the environment, of resources and of the climate, require all international leaders to act jointly and to show a readiness to work in good faith, respecting the law, and promoting solidarity with the weakest regions of the planet. I am thinking especially of those countries in Africa and other parts of the world which remain on the margins of authentic integral development, and are therefore at risk of experiencing only the negative effects of globalization. In the context of international relations, it is necessary to recognize the higher role played by rules and structures that are intrinsically ordered to promote the common good, and therefore to safeguard human freedom. These regulations do not limit freedom. On the contrary, they promote it when they prohibit behavior and actions which work against the common good, curb its effective exercise and hence compromise the dignity of every human person. In the name of freedom, there has to be a correlation between rights and duties, by which every person is called to assume responsibility for his or her choices, made as a consequence of entering into relations with others. Here our thoughts turn also to the way the results of scientific research and technological advances have sometimes been applied. Notwithstanding the enormous benefits that humanity can gain, some instances of this represent a clear violation of the order of creation, to the point where not only is the sacred character of life contradicted, but the human person and the family are robbed of their natural identity. Likewise, international action to preserve the environment and to protect various forms of life on earth must not only guarantee a rational use of technology and science, but must also rediscover the authentic image of creation. This never requires a choice to be made between science and ethics: rather it is a question of adopting a scientific method that is truly respectful of ethical imperatives.

Recognition of the unity of the human family, and attention to the innate dignity of every man and woman, today find renewed emphasis in the principle of the responsibility to protect. This has only recently been defined, but it was already present implicitly at the origins of the United Nations, and is now increasingly characteristic of its activity. Every State has the primary duty to protect its own population from grave and sustained violations of human rights, as well as from the consequences of humanitarian crises, whether natural or man-made. If States are unable to guarantee such protection, the international community must intervene with the juridical means provided in the United Nations Charter and in other international instruments. The action of the international community and its institutions, provided that it respects the principles undergirding the international order, should never be interpreted as an unwarranted imposition or a limitation of sovereignty. On the contrary, it is indifference or failure to intervene that do the real damage. What is needed is a deeper search for ways of pre-empting and managing conflicts by exploring every possible diplomatic avenue, and giving attention and encouragement to even the faintest sign of dialogue or desire for reconciliation.

The principle of "responsibility to protect" was considered by the ancient *ius gentium* as the foundation of every action taken by those in government with regard to the governed: at the time when the concept of national sovereign States was first developing, the Dominican Friar Francisco de Vitoria, rightly considered as a precursor of the idea of the United Nations, described this responsibility as an aspect of natural reason shared by all nations, and the result of an international order whose task it was to regulate relations between peoples. Now, as then, this principle has to invoke the idea of the person as image of the Creator, the desire for the absolute and the essence of freedom. The founding of the United Nations, as we know, coincided with the profound upheavals that humanity experienced when reference to the meaning of transcendence and natural reason was abandoned, and in consequence, freedom and human dignity were grossly violated. When this happens, it threatens the objective foundations of the values inspiring and governing the international order and it undermines the cogent and inviolable principles formulated and consolidated by the United Nations. When faced with new and insistent challenges, it is a mistake to fall back on a pragmatic approach, limited to determining "common ground", minimal in content and weak in its effect.

This reference to human dignity, which is the foundation and goal of the responsibility to protect, leads us to the theme we are specifically focusing upon this year, which marks the sixtieth anniversary of the Universal Declaration of Human Rights. This document was the outcome of a convergence of different religious and cultural traditions, all of them motivated by the common desire to place the human person at the heart of institutions, laws and the workings of society, and to consider the human person essential for the world of culture, religion and science. Human rights are increasingly being presented as the common language and the ethical substratum of international relations. At the same time, the universality, indivisibility and interdependence of human rights all serve as guarantees safeguarding human dignity. It is evident, though, that the rights recognized and expounded in the Declaration apply to everyone by virtue of the common origin of the person, who remains the highpoint of God's creative design for the world and for history. They are based on the natural law inscribed on human hearts and present in different cultures and civilizations. Removing human rights from this context would mean restricting their range and yielding to a relativistic conception, according to which the meaning and interpretation of rights could vary and their universality would be denied in the name of different cultural, political, social and even religious outlooks.

This great variety of viewpoints must not be allowed to obscure the fact that not only rights are universal, but so too is the human person, the subject of those rights.

The life of the community, both domestically and internationally, clearly demonstrates that respect for rights, and the guarantees that follow from them, are measures of the common good that serve to evaluate the relationship between justice and injustice, development and poverty, security and conflict. The promotion of human rights remains the most effective strategy for eliminating inequalities between countries and social groups, and for increasing security. Indeed, the victims of hardship and despair, whose human dignity is violated with impunity, become easy prey to the call to violence, and they can then become violators of peace. The common good that human rights help to accomplish cannot, however, be attained merely by applying correct procedures, nor even less by achieving a balance between competing rights. The merit of the Universal Declaration is that it has enabled different cultures, juridical expressions and institutional models to converge around a fundamental nucleus of values, and hence of rights. Today, though, efforts need to be redoubled in the face of pressure to reinterpret the foundations of the Declaration and to compromise its inner unity so as to facilitate a move away from the protection of human dignity towards the satisfaction of simple interests, often particular interests. The Declaration was adopted as a "common standard of achievement" (Preamble) and cannot be applied piecemeal, according to trends or selective choices that merely run the risk of contradicting the unity of the human person and thus the indivisibility of human rights.

Experience shows that legality often prevails over justice when the insistence upon rights makes them appear as the exclusive result of legislative enactments or normative decisions taken by the various agencies of those in power.

When presented purely in terms of legality, rights risk becoming weak propositions divorced from the ethical and rational dimension which is their foundation and their goal. The Universal Declaration, rather, has reinforced the conviction that respect for human rights is principally rooted in unchanging justice, on which the binding force of international proclamations is also based. This aspect is often overlooked when the attempt is made to deprive rights of their true function in the name of a narrowly utilitarian perspective. Since rights and the resulting duties follow naturally from human interaction, it is easy to forget that they are the fruit of a commonly held sense of justice built primarily upon solidarity among the members of society, and hence valid at all times and for all peoples. This intuition was expressed as early as the fifth century by Augustine of Hippo, one of the masters of our intellectual heritage. He taught that the saying: *Do not do to others what you would not want done to you* "cannot in any way vary according to the different understandings that have arisen in the world" (*De Doctrina Christiana*, III, 14). Human rights, then, must be respected as an expression of justice, and not merely because they are enforceable through the will of the legislators.

LADIES AND GENTLEMEN,

As history proceeds, new situations arise, and the attempt is made to link them to new rights. Discernment, that is, the capacity to distinguish good from evil, becomes even more essential in the context of demands that concern the very lives and conduct of persons, communities and peoples. In tackling the theme of rights, since important situations and profound realities are involved, discernment is both an indispensable and a fruitful virtue.

Discernment, then, shows that entrusting exclusively to individual States, with their laws and institutions, the final responsibility to meet the aspirations of persons, communities and entire peoples, can sometimes have consequences that exclude the possibility of a social order respectful of the dignity and rights of the person. On the other hand, a vision of life firmly anchored in the religious dimension can help to achieve this, since recognition of the transcendent value of every man and woman favors conversion of heart, which then leads to a commitment to resist violence, terrorism and war, and to promote justice and peace. This also provides the proper context for the interreligious dialogue that the United Nations is called to support, just as it supports dialogue in other areas of human activity. Dialogue should be recognized as the means by which the various components of society can articulate their point of view and build consensus around the truth concerning particular values or goals. It pertains to the nature of religions, freely practiced, that they can autonomously conduct a dialogue of thought and life. If at this level, too, the religious sphere is kept separate from political action, then great benefits ensue for individuals and communities. On the other hand, the United Nations can count on the results of dialogue between religions, and can draw fruit from the willingness of believers to place their experiences at the service of the common good. Their task is to propose a vision of faith not in terms of intolerance, discrimination and conflict, but in terms of complete respect for truth, coexistence, rights, and reconciliation.

Human rights, of course, must include the right to religious freedom, understood as the expression of a dimension that is at once individual and communitarian—a vision that brings out the unity of the person while clearly distinguishing between the dimension of the citizen and that of the believer. The activity of the United Nations in recent years has ensured that public debate gives space to viewpoints inspired by a religious vision in all its dimensions, including ritual, worship, education, dissemination of information and the freedom to profess and choose religion. It is inconceivable, then, that believers should have to suppress a part of themselves—their faith—in order to be active citizens. It should never be necessary to deny God in order to enjoy one's rights. The rights associated with religion are all the more in need of protection if they are considered to clash with a prevailing secular ideology or with majority religious positions of an exclusive nature. The full guarantee of religious liberty cannot be limited to the free exercise of worship, but has to give due consideration to the public dimension of religion, and hence to the possibility of believers playing their part in building the social order. Indeed, they actually do so, for example through their influential and generous involvement in a vast network of initiatives which extend from Universities, scientific institutions and schools to health care agencies and charitable organizations in the service of the poorest and most marginalized. Refusal to recognize the contribution to society that is rooted in the religious dimension and in the quest for the Absolute—by its nature, expressing communion between persons—would effectively privilege an individualistic approach, and would fragment the unity of the person.

My presence at this Assembly is a sign of esteem for the United Nations, and it is intended to express the hope that the Organization will increasingly serve as a sign of unity between States and an instrument of service to the entire human family. It also demonstrates the willingness of the Catholic Church to offer her proper contribution to building international relations in a way that allows every person and every people to feel they can make a difference. In a manner that is consistent with her contribution in the ethical and moral sphere and the free activity of her faithful, the Church also works for the realization of these goals through the international activity of the Holy See. Indeed, the Holy See has always had a place at the assemblies of the Nations, thereby manifesting its specific character as a subject in the international domain. As the United Nations recently confirmed, the Holy See thereby makes its contribution according to the dispositions of international law, helps to define that law, and makes appeal to it.

The United Nations remains a privileged setting in which the Church is committed to contributing her experience "of humanity", developed over the centuries among peoples of every race and culture, and placing it at the disposal of all members of the international community. This experience and activity, directed towards attaining freedom for every believer, seeks also to increase the protection given to the rights of the person. Those rights are grounded and shaped by the transcendent nature of the person, which permits men and women to pursue their journey of faith and their search for God in this world. Recognition of this dimension must be strengthened if we are to sustain humanity's hope for a better world and if we are to create the conditions for peace, development, cooperation, and guarantee of rights for future generations.

In my recent Encyclical, *Spe Salvi*, I indicated that "every generation has the task of engaging anew in the arduous search for the right way to order human affairs" (no. 25). For Christians, this task is motivated by the hope drawn from the saving work of Jesus Christ. That is why the Church is happy to be associated with the activity of this distinguished Organization, charged with the responsibility of promoting peace and good will throughout the earth. Dear Friends, I thank you for this opportunity to address you today, and I promise you of the support of my prayers as you pursue your noble task.

Before I take my leave from this distinguished Assembly, I should like to offer my greetings, in the official languages, to all the Nations here represented.

Peace and Prosperity with God's help!

Paix et prospérité, avec l'aide de Dieu!

Paz y prosperidad con la ayuda de Dios!

Thank you very much.

Shepherd One arrives at Andrews Air Force Base in Maryland, just outside Washington, D.C., April 15, 2008.

Papal address at welcoming ceremony on the South Lawn of the White House, April 16, 2008.

Most Rev. Alfred C. Hughes, Archbishop of New Orleans, is presented with the gift of a chalice for the archdiocese in honor of the rebuilding efforts after Hurricane Katrina in 2005. Vatican Secretary of State Cardinal Tarcisio Bertone applauds as Pope Benedict XVI makes this presentation at the Basilica of the National Shrine of the Immaculate Conception, Washington, D.C., April 16, 2008.

Pope greeting the crowds after Mass at Nationals Park, Washington, D.C., April 17, 2008.

Bishop Jongmae Kenneth Park of the Korean Buddhist Taego Order greets Pope Benedict XVI during an interfaith gathering at the Pope John Paul II Cultural Center, Washington, D.C., April 17, 2008.

Saman Hussain presents the Pope with a book containing poetic verses from the Koran, the holy book of Islam, during an interfaith gathering at the Pope John Paul II Cultural Center of Washington, D.C., April 17, 2008. The Pope's private secretary, Msgr. Georg Ganswein, looks on.

Pope Benedict XVI addresses the United Nations General Assembly in New York, April 18, 2008.

The pope greets families upon his arrival at St. Joseph's Church in New York prior to the ecumenical prayer service, April 18, 2008.

Archbishop Demetrios, primate of the Greek Orthodox Church in America, meets with Pope Benedict XVI during an ecumenical prayer service at St. Joseph's Church, New York, April 18, 2008.

The Pope-mobile passes in front of St. Patrick's Cathedral and makes its way up 5th Avenue, April 19, 2008.

Pope Benedict XVI greets young people and seminarians at St. Joseph's Seminary, Yonkers, New York, April 19, 2008.

Farewell address to a crowd gathered in a hangar at John Fitzgerald Kennedy International Airport, New York, April 20, 2008.

A commemorative medallion of the apostolic journey.

GREETINGS OF
HIS HOLINESS BENEDICT XVI
TO THE STAFF OF THE
UNITED NATIONS

New York
Friday, April 18, 2008

LADIES AND GENTLEMEN,

Here, within a small space in the busy city of New York, is housed an Organization with a worldwide mission to promote peace and justice. I am reminded of the similar contrast in scale between Vatican City State and the world in which the Church exercises her universal mission and apostolate. The sixteenth-century artists who painted the maps on the walls of the Apostolic Palace reminded the Popes of the vast extent of the known world. In those frescoes, the Successors of Peter were offered a tangible sign of the immense outreach of the Church's mission at a time when the discovery of the New World was opening up unforeseen horizons. Here in this glass palace, the art on display has its own way of reminding us of the responsibilities of the United Nations Organization. We see images of the effects of war and poverty, we are reminded of our duty to strive for a better world, and we rejoice in the sheer diversity and exuberance of human culture, manifested in the wide range of peoples and nations gathered together under the umbrella of the international community.

On the occasion of my visit, I wish to pay tribute to the invaluable contribution made by the administrative staff and the many employees of the United Nations, who carry out their duties with such great dedication and professionalism every day—here in New York, in other U.N. centers, and at special missions all over the world. To you, and to those who have gone before you, I would like to express my personal appreciation and that of the whole Catholic Church. We remember especially the many civilians and peace-keepers who have sacrificed their lives in the field for the good of the peoples they serve—in 2007 alone there were forty-two of them. We also remember the vast multitude who dedicate their lives to work that is never sufficiently acknowledged, often in difficult circumstances. To all of you—translators, secretaries, administrative personnel of every kind, maintenance and security staff, development workers, peace-keepers and many others—thank you, most sincerely. The work that you do makes it possible for the Organization to continue exploring new ways of achieving the goals for which it was founded.

The United Nations is often spoken of as the "family of nations". By the same token, the headquarters here in New York could be described as a home, a place of welcome and concern for the good of family members everywhere. It is an excellent place in which to promote growth in understanding and collaboration between peoples. Rightly, the staff of the United Nations are selected from a wide range of cultures and nationalities. The personnel here constitute a microcosm of the whole world, in which each individual makes an indispensable contribution from the perspective of his or her particular cultural and religious heritage. The ideals that inspired the founders of this institution need to take shape here and in every one of the Organization's missions around the world in the mutual respect and acceptance that are the hallmarks of a thriving family.

In the internal debates of the United Nations, increasing emphasis is being placed on the "responsibility to protect". Indeed this is coming to be recognized as the moral basis for a government's claim to authority. It is also a feature that naturally appertains to a family, in which stronger members take care of weaker ones. This Organization performs an important service, in the name of the international community, by monitoring the extent to which governments fulfill their responsibility to protect their citizens. On a day-to-day level, it is you who lay the foundations on which that work is built, by the concern you show for one another in the workplace, and by your solicitude for the many peoples whose needs and aspirations you serve in all that you do.

The Catholic Church, through the international activity of the Holy See, and through countless initiatives of lay Catholics, local Churches and religious communities, assures you of her support for your work. I assure you and your families of a special remembrance in my prayers. May Almighty God bless you always and comfort you with his grace and his peace, so that through the care you offer to the entire human family, you can continue to be of service to him.

Thank you.

WORDS OF
HIS HOLINESS BENEDICT XVI
TO THE PARK EAST
SYNAGOGUE

PARK EAST SYNAGOGUE,
NEW YORK
Friday, April 18, 2008

DEAR FRIENDS,

Shalom! It is with joy that I come here, just a few hours before the celebration of your *Pesah*, to express my respect and esteem for the Jewish community in New York City. The proximity of this place of worship to my residence gives me the opportunity to greet some of you today. I find it moving to recall that Jesus, as a young boy, heard the words of Scripture and prayed in a place such as this. I thank Rabbi Schneier for his words of welcome and I particularly appreciate your kind gift, the spring flowers and the lovely song that the children sang for me. I know that the Jewish community make a valuable contribution to the life of the city, and I encourage all of you to continue building bridges of friendship with all the many different ethnic and religious groups present in your neighborhood. I assure you most especially of my closeness at this time, as you prepare to celebrate the great deeds of the Almighty, and to sing the praises of Him who has worked such wonders for his people. I would ask those of you who are present to pass on my greetings and good wishes to all the members of the Jewish community. Blessed be the name of the Lord!

ADDRESS OF HIS HOLINESS BENEDICT XVI DURING ECUMENICAL PRAYER SERVICE

St. Joseph's Parish, New York
Friday, April 18, 2008

DEAR BROTHERS AND SISTERS IN CHRIST,

My heart abounds with gratitude to Almighty God—
"the Father of all, who is over all and through all and in all"
(*Eph* 4:6)—for this blessed opportunity to gather with you
this evening in prayer. I thank Bishop Dennis Sullivan for his
cordial welcome, and I warmly greet all those in attendance
representing Christian communities throughout the United
States. May the peace of our Lord and Savior be with you all!

Through you, I express my sincere appreciation for the
invaluable work of all those engaged in ecumenism: the
National Council of Churches, Christian Churches Together,
the Catholic Bishops' Secretariat for Ecumenical and Interreligious Affairs, and many others. The contribution of
Christians in the United States to the ecumenical movement
is felt throughout the world. I encourage all of you to persevere, always relying on the grace of the risen Christ whom we
strive to serve by bringing about "the obedience of faith for
the sake of his name" (*Rom* 1:5).

We have just listened to the scriptural passage in which Paul—a "prisoner for the Lord"—delivers his ardent appeal to the members of the Christian community at Ephesus. "I beg you," he writes, "to lead a life worthy of the calling to which you have been called...eager to maintain the unity of the Spirit in the bond of peace" (*Eph* 4:1–3). Then, after his impassioned litany of unity, Paul reminds his hearers that Jesus, having ascended into heaven, has bestowed upon men and women all the gifts necessary for building up the Body of Christ (cf. *Eph* 4:11–13).

Paul's exhortation resounds with no less vigor today. His words instill in us the confidence that the Lord will never abandon us in our quest for unity. They also call us to live in a way that bears witness to the "one heart and mind" (*Acts* 4:32), which has always been the distinguishing trait of Christian *koinonia* (cf. *Acts* 2:42), and the force drawing others to join the community of believers so that they too might come to share in the "unsearchable riches of Christ" (*Eph* 3:8; cf. *Acts* 2:47, 5:14).

Globalization has humanity poised between two poles. On the one hand, there is a growing sense of interconnectedness and interdependency between peoples even when—geographically and culturally speaking—they are far apart. This new situation offers the potential for enhancing a sense of global solidarity and shared responsibility for the well-being of mankind. On the other hand, we cannot deny that the rapid changes occurring in our world also present some disturbing signs of fragmentation and a retreat into individualism. The expanding use of electronic communications has in some cases paradoxically resulted in greater isolation. Many people—including the young—are seeking therefore more authentic forms of community. Also of grave concern is the spread of a secularist ideology that undermines or even rejects transcendent truth. The very possibility of divine revelation, and therefore of Christian faith, is often placed into question by cultural trends widely present in academia, the mass media and public debate. For these reasons, a faithful witness to the Gospel is as urgent as ever. Christians are challenged to give a clear account of the hope that they hold (cf. 1 *Pet* 3:15).

Too often those who are not Christians, as they observe the splintering of Christian communities, are understandably confused about the Gospel message itself. Fundamental Christian beliefs and practices are sometimes changed within communities by so-called "prophetic actions" that are based on a hermeneutic not always consonant with the datum of Scripture and Tradition. Communities consequently give up the attempt to act as a unified body, choosing instead to function according to the idea of "local options". Somewhere in this process the need for *diachronic koinonia*—communion with the Church in every age—is lost, just at the time when the world is losing its bearings and needs a persuasive common witness to the saving power of the Gospel (cf. *Rom* 1:18–23).

Faced with these difficulties, we must first recall that the unity of the Church flows from the perfect oneness of the triune God. In John's Gospel, we are told that Jesus prayed to his Father that his disciples might be one, "just as you are in me and I am in you" (*John* 17:21). This passage reflects the unwavering conviction of the early Christian community that its unity was both caused by, and is reflective of, the unity of the Father, Son, and Holy Spirit. This, in turn, suggests that the internal cohesion of believers was based on the sound integrity of their doctrinal confession (cf. 1 *Tim* 1:3–11). Throughout the New Testament, we find that the Apostles were repeatedly called to give an account for their faith to both Gentiles (cf. *Acts* 17:16–34) and Jews (cf. *Acts* 4:5–22, 5:27–42). The core of their argument was always the historical fact of Jesus' bodily resurrection from the tomb (*Acts*

2:24, 32; 3:15; 4:10; 5:30; 10:40; 13:30). The ultimate effectiveness of their preaching did not depend on "lofty words" or "human wisdom" (1 *Cor* 2:13), but rather on the work of the Spirit (*Eph* 3:5) who confirmed the authoritative witness of the Apostles (cf. 1 *Cor* 15:1–11). The nucleus of Paul's preaching and that of the early Church was none other than Jesus Christ, and "him crucified" (1 *Cor* 2:2). But this proclamation had to be guaranteed by the purity of normative doctrine expressed in creedal formulae—*symbola*—which articulated the essence of the Christian faith and constituted the foundation for the unity of the baptized (cf. 1 *Cor* 15:3–5, 1:6–9; *Unitatis Redintegratio*, 2).

My dear friends, the power of the *kerygma* has lost none of its internal dynamism. Yet we must ask ourselves whether its full force has not been attenuated by a relativistic approach to Christian doctrine similar to that found in secular ideologies, which, in alleging that science alone is "objective", relegate religion entirely to the subjective sphere of individual feeling. Scientific discoveries, and their application through human ingenuity, undoubtedly offer new possibilities for the betterment of humankind. This does not mean, however, that the "knowable" is limited to the empirically verifiable, nor religion restricted to the shifting realm of "personal experience".

For Christians to accept this faulty line of reasoning would lead to the notion that there is little need to emphasize objective truth in the presentation of the Christian faith, for one need but follow his or her own conscience and choose a community that best suits his or her individual tastes. The result is seen in the continual proliferation of communities which often eschew institutional structures and minimize the importance of doctrinal content for Christian living.

Even within the ecumenical movement, Christians may be reluctant to assert the role of doctrine for fear that it would only exacerbate rather than heal the wounds of division. Yet a clear, convincing testimony to the salvation wrought for us in Christ Jesus has to be based upon the notion of normative apostolic teaching: a teaching which indeed underlies the inspired word of God and sustains the sacramental life of Christians today.

Only by "holding fast" to sound teaching (2 *Thess* 2:15; cf. *Rev* 2:12–29) will we be able to respond to the challenges that confront us in an evolving world. Only in this way will we give unambiguous testimony to the truth of the Gospel and its moral teaching. This is the message which the world is waiting to hear from us. Like the early Christians, we have a responsibility to give transparent witness to the "reasons for our hope", so that the eyes of all men and women of goodwill may be opened to see that God has shown us his face (cf. 2 *Cor* 3:12–18) and granted us access to his divine life through Jesus Christ. He alone is our hope! God has revealed his love for all peoples through the mystery of his Son's passion and death, and has called us to proclaim that he is indeed risen, has taken his place at the right hand of the Father, and "will come again in glory to judge the living and the dead" *(Nicene Creed)*.

May the word of God we have heard this evening inflame our hearts with hope on the path to unity (cf. *Luke* 24:32). May this prayer service exemplify the centrality of prayer in the ecumenical movement (cf. *Unitatis Redintegratio,* 8); for without it, ecumenical structures, institutions and programs would be deprived of their heart and soul. Let us give thanks to Almighty God for the progress that has been made through the work of his Spirit, as we acknowledge with gratitude the personal sacrifices made by so many present and by those who have gone before us.

By following in their footsteps, and by placing our trust in God alone, I am confident that—to borrow the words of

Father Paul Wattson—we will achieve the "oneness of hope, oneness of faith, and oneness of love" that alone will convince the world that Jesus Christ is the one sent by the Father for the salvation of all.

I thank you all.

HOMILY OF
HIS HOLINESS BENEDICT XVI
DURING A VOTIVE MASS
FOR THE UNIVERSAL CHURCH AT
ST. PATRICK'S CATHEDRAL

ST. PATRICK'S CATHEDRAL, NEW YORK
Saturday, April 19, 2008

DEAR BROTHERS AND SISTERS IN CHRIST,

With great affection in the Lord, I greet all of you, who represent the Bishops, priests and deacons, the men and women in consecrated life, and the seminarians of the United States. I thank Cardinal Egan for his warm welcome and the good wishes which he has expressed in your name as I begin the fourth year of my papal ministry. I am happy to celebrate this Mass with you, who have been chosen by the Lord, who have answered his call, and who devote your lives to the pursuit of holiness, the spread of the Gospel and the building up of the Church in faith, hope and love.

Gathered as we are in this historic cathedral, how can we not think of the countless men and women who have gone before us, who labored for the growth of the Church in the United States, and left us a lasting legacy of faith and good works? In today's first reading we saw how, in the power of the Holy Spirit, the Apostles went forth from the Upper Room to proclaim God's mighty works to people of every nation and tongue. In this country, the Church's mission has always involved drawing people "from every nation under heaven" (cf. *Acts* 2:5) into spiritual unity, and enriching the Body of Christ by the variety of their gifts. As we give thanks for these precious past blessings, and look to the challenges of the future, let us implore from God the grace of a new Pentecost for the Church in America. May tongues of fire, combining burning love of God and neighbor with zeal for the spread of Christ's Kingdom, descend on all present!

In this morning's second reading, Saint Paul reminds us that spiritual unity—the unity which reconciles and enriches diversity—has its origin and supreme model in the life of the triune God. As a communion of pure love and infinite freedom, the Blessed Trinity constantly brings forth new life in the work of creation and redemption. The Church, as "a people made one by the unity of the Father, the Son and the Spirit" (cf. *Lumen Gentium*, 4), is called to proclaim the gift of life, to serve life, and to promote a culture of life. Here in this cathedral, our thoughts turn naturally to the heroic witness to the Gospel of life borne by the late Cardinals Cooke and O'Connor. The proclamation of life, life in abundance, must be the heart of the new evangelization. For true life— our salvation—can only be found in the reconciliation, freedom and love which are God's gracious gift.

This is the message of hope we are called to proclaim and embody in a world where self-centeredness, greed, violence, and cynicism so often seem to choke the fragile growth of grace in people's hearts. Saint Irenaeus, with great insight, understood that the command which Moses enjoined upon the people of Israel: "Choose life!" (*Deut* 30:19) was the ultimate reason for our obedience to all God's commandments (cf. *Adv. Haer.* IV, 16, 2–5). Perhaps we have lost sight of this: in a society where the Church seems legalistic and "institutional" to many people, our most urgent challenge is to communicate the joy born of faith and the experience of God's love.

I am particularly happy that we have gathered in Saint Patrick's Cathedral. Perhaps more than any other church in the United States, this place is known and loved as "a house of prayer for all peoples" (cf. *Isa* 56:7; *Mark* 11:17). Each day thousands of men, women and children enter its doors and find peace within its walls. Archbishop John Hughes, who—as Cardinal Egan has reminded us—was responsible for building this venerable edifice, wished it to rise in pure Gothic style. He wanted this cathedral to remind the young Church in America of the great spiritual tradition to which it was heir, and to inspire it to bring the best of that heritage to the building up of Christ's body in this land. I would like to draw your attention to a few aspects of this beautiful structure which I think can serve as a starting point for a reflection on our particular vocations within the unity of the Mystical Body.

The first has to do with the stained glass windows, which flood the interior with mystic light. From the outside, those windows are dark, heavy, even dreary. But once one enters the church, they suddenly come alive; reflecting the light passing through them, they reveal all their splendor. Many writers—here in America we can think of Nathaniel Hawthorne—have used the image of stained glass to illustrate the mystery of the Church herself. It is only from the inside, from the experience of faith and ecclesial life, that we see the Church as she truly is: flooded with grace, resplendent in beauty, adorned by the manifold gifts of the Spirit. It follows that we, who live the life of grace within the Church's communion, are called to draw all people into this mystery of light.

This is no easy task in a world which can tend to look at the Church, like those stained glass windows, "from the outside": a world which deeply senses a need for spirituality, yet finds it difficult to "enter into" the mystery of the Church. Even for those of us within, the light of faith can be dimmed by routine, and the splendor of the Church obscured by the sins and weaknesses of her members. It can be dimmed too, by the obstacles encountered in a society which sometimes seems to have forgotten God and to resent even the most elementary demands of Christian morality. You, who have devoted your lives to bearing witness to the love of Christ and the building up of his Body, know from your daily contact with the world around us how tempting it is at times to give way to frustration, disappointment and even pessimism about the future. In a word, it is not always easy to see the light of the Spirit all about us, the splendor of the Risen Lord illuminating our lives and instilling renewed hope in his victory over the world (cf. *John* 16:33).

Yet the word of God reminds us that, in faith, we see the heavens opened, and the grace of the Holy Spirit lighting up the Church and bringing sure hope to our world. "O Lord, my God," the Psalmist sings, "when you send forth your spirit, they are created, and you renew the face of the earth" (*Ps* 104:30). These words evoke the first creation, when the Spirit of God hovered over the deep (cf. *Gen* 1:2). And they look forward to the new creation, at Pentecost, when the Holy Spirit descended upon the Apostles and established the Church as the first fruits of a redeemed humanity (cf. *John* 20:22–23). These words summon us to ever deeper faith in God's infinite power to transform every human situation, to create life from death, and to light up even the darkest night. And they make us think of another magnificent phrase of

Saint Irenaeus: "where the Church is, there is the Spirit of God; where the Spirit of God is, there is the Church and all grace" (*Adv. Haer.* III, 24, 1).

This leads me to a further reflection about the architecture of this church. Like all Gothic cathedrals, it is a highly complex structure, whose exact and harmonious proportions symbolize the unity of God's creation. Medieval artists often portrayed Christ, the creative Word of God, as a heavenly "geometer", compass in hand, who orders the cosmos with infinite wisdom and purpose. Does this not bring to mind our need to see all things with the eyes of faith, and thus to grasp them in their truest perspective, in the unity of God's eternal plan? This requires, as we know, constant conversion, and a commitment to acquiring "a fresh, spiritual way of thinking" (cf. *Eph* 4:23). It also calls for the cultivation of those virtues which enable each of us to grow in holiness and to bear spiritual fruit within our particular state of life. Is not this ongoing "intellectual" conversion as necessary as "moral" conversion for our own growth in faith, our discernment of the signs of the times, and our personal contribution to the Church's life and mission?

For all of us, I think, one of the great disappointments which followed the Second Vatican Council, with its call for a greater engagement in the Church's mission to the world, has been the experience of division between different groups, different generations, different members of the same religious family. We can only move forward if we turn our gaze together to Christ! In the light of faith, we will then discover the wisdom and strength needed to open ourselves to points of view which may not necessarily conform to our own ideas or assumptions. Thus we can value the perspectives of others, be they younger or older than ourselves, and ultimately hear "what the Spirit is saying" to us and to the Church (cf. *Rev* 2:7). In this way, we will move together towards that true spiritual renewal desired by the Council, a renewal which can only strengthen the Church in that holiness and unity indispensable for the effective proclamation of the Gospel in today's world.

Was not this unity of vision and purpose—rooted in faith and a spirit of constant conversion and self-sacrifice— the secret of the impressive growth of the Church in this country? We need but think of the remarkable accomplishment of that exemplary American priest, the Venerable Michael McGivney, whose vision and zeal led to the establishment of the Knights of Columbus, or of the legacy of the generations of religious and priests who quietly devoted their lives to serving the People of God in countless schools, hospitals and parishes.

Here, within the context of our need for the perspective given by faith, and for unity and cooperation in the work of building up the Church, I would like say a word about the sexual abuse that has caused so much suffering. I have already had occasion to speak of this, and of the resulting damage to the community of the faithful. Here I simply wish to assure you, dear priests and religious, of my spiritual closeness as you strive to respond with Christian hope to the continuing challenges that this situation presents. I join you in praying that this will be a time of purification for each and every particular Church and religious community, and a time for healing. And I also encourage you to cooperate with your Bishops who continue to work effectively to resolve this issue. May our Lord Jesus Christ grant the Church in America a renewed sense of unity and purpose, as all—Bishops, clergy, religious and laity—move forward in hope, in love for the truth and for one another.

Dear friends, these considerations lead me to a final observation about this great cathedral in which we find ourselves. The unity of a Gothic cathedral, we know, is not the static unity of a classical temple, but a unity born of the dynamic tension of diverse forces which impel the architecture upward, pointing it to heaven. Here too, we can see a symbol of the Church's unity, which is the unity—as Saint Paul has told us—of a living body composed of many different members, each with its own role and purpose. Here too we see our need to acknowledge and reverence the gifts of each and every member of the body as "manifestations of the Spirit given for the good of all" (1 *Cor* 12:7). Certainly within the Church's divinely-willed structure there is a distinction to be made between hierarchical and charismatic gifts (cf. *Lumen Gentium*, 4). Yet the very variety and richness of the graces bestowed by the Spirit invite us constantly to discern how these gifts are to be rightly ordered in the service of the Church's mission. You, dear priests, by sacramental ordination have been configured to Christ, the Head of the Body. You, dear deacons, have been ordained for the service of that Body. You, dear men and women religious, both contemplative and apostolic, have devoted your lives to following the divine Master in generous love and complete devotion to his Gospel. All of you, who fill this cathedral today, as well as your retired, elderly and infirm brothers and sisters, who unite their prayers and sacrifices to your labors, are called to be forces of unity within Christ's Body. By your personal witness, and your fidelity to the ministry or apostolate entrusted to you, you prepare a path for the Spirit. For the Spirit never ceases to pour out his abundant gifts, to awaken new vocations and missions, and to guide the Church, as our Lord promised in this morning's Gospel, into the fullness of truth (cf. *John* 16:13).

So let us lift our gaze upward! And with great humility and confidence, let us ask the Spirit to enable us each day to grow in the holiness that will make us living stones in the temple which he is even now raising up in the midst of our world. If we are to be true forces of unity, let us be the first to seek inner reconciliation through penance. Let us forgive the wrongs we have suffered and put aside all anger and contention. Let us be the first to demonstrate the humility and purity of heart which are required to approach the splendor of God's truth. In fidelity to the deposit of faith entrusted to the Apostles (cf. 1 *Tim* 6:20), let us be joyful witnesses of the transforming power of the Gospel!

Dear brothers and sisters, in the finest traditions of the Church in this country, may you also be the first friend of the poor, the homeless, the stranger, the sick and all who suffer. Act as beacons of hope, casting the light of Christ upon the world, and encouraging young people to discover the beauty of a life given completely to the Lord and his Church. I make this plea in a particular way to the many seminarians and young religious present. All of you have a special place in my heart. Never forget that you are called to carry on, with all the enthusiasm and joy that the Spirit has given you, a work that others have begun, a legacy that one day you too will have to pass on to a new generation. Work generously and joyfully, for he whom you serve is the Lord!

The spires of Saint Patrick's Cathedral are dwarfed by the skyscrapers of the Manhattan skyline, yet in the heart of this busy metropolis, they are a vivid reminder of the constant yearning of the human spirit to rise to God. As we celebrate this Eucharist, let us thank the Lord for allowing us to know him in the communion of the Church, to cooperate in building up his Mystical Body, and in bringing his saving word as good news to the men and women of our time. And when we leave this great church, let us go forth as heralds of hope in the midst of this city, and all those places where God's grace has placed us. In this way, the Church in America will know a new springtime in the Spirit, and point the way to that other, greater city, the new Jerusalem, whose light is the Lamb (*Rev* 21:23). For there God is even now preparing for all people a banquet of unending joy and life. Amen.

WORDS SPOKEN SPONTANEOUSLY BY THE HOLY FATHER AT THE CONCLUSION OF THE HOLY MASS:

At this moment I can only thank you for your love of the Church and Our Lord, and for the love which you show to the poor Successor of Saint Peter. I will try to do all that is possible to be a worthy successor of the great Apostle, who also was a man with faults and sins, but remained in the end the rock for the Church. And so I too, with all my spiritual poverty, can be for this time, in virtue of the Lord's grace, the Successor of Peter.

It is also your prayers and your love which give me the certainty that the Lord will help me in this my ministry. I am therefore deeply grateful for your love and for your prayers. My response now for all that you have given to me during this visit is my blessing, which I impart to you at the conclusion of this beautiful Celebration.

WORDS OF HIS HOLINESS BENEDICT XVI TO YOUNG PEOPLE HAVING DISABILITIES

SAINT JOSEPH'S SEMINARY, YONKERS, NEW YORK
Saturday, April 19, 2008

YOUR EMINENCE,

BISHOP WALSH,

DEAR FRIENDS,

I am very happy to have this opportunity to spend a brief moment with you. I thank Cardinal Egan for his welcome and especially thank your representatives for their kind words and for the gift of the drawing. Know that it is a special joy for me to be with you. Please give my greetings to your parents and family members, and your teachers and caregivers.

God has blessed you with life, and with differing talents and gifts. Through these you are able to serve him and society in various ways. While some people's contributions seem great and others' more modest, the witness value of our efforts is always a sign of hope for everyone.

Sometimes it is challenging to find a reason for what appears only as a difficulty to be overcome or even pain to be endured. Yet our faith helps us to break open the horizon beyond our own selves in order to see life as God does. God's unconditional love, which bathes every human individual, points to a meaning and purpose for all human life. Through his Cross, Jesus in fact draws us into his saving love (cf. *John* 12:32) and in so doing shows us the way ahead—the way of hope which transfigures us all, so that we too, become bearers of that hope and charity for others.

Dear friends, I encourage you all to pray every day for our world. There are so many intentions and people you can pray for, including those who have yet to come to know Jesus. And please do continue to pray for me. As you know I have just had another birthday. Time passes!

Thank you all again, including the Cathedral of Saint Patrick Young Singers and the members of the Archdiocesan Deaf Choir. As a sign of strength and peace and with great affection in our Lord, I impart to you and your families, teachers and caregivers my Apostolic Blessing.

ADDRESS OF HIS HOLINESS BENEDICT XVI TO YOUNG PEOPLE AND SEMINARIANS

Saint Joseph's Seminary, Yonkers, New York
Saturday, April 19, 2008

YOUR EMINENCE,

DEAR BROTHER BISHOPS,

DEAR YOUNG FRIENDS,

"Proclaim the Lord Christ...and always have your answer ready for people who ask the reason for the hope that is within you" (1 *Pet* 3:15). With these words from the *First Letter of Peter* I greet each of you with heartfelt affection. I thank Cardinal Egan for his kind words of welcome and I also thank the representatives chosen from among you for their gestures of welcome. To Bishop Walsh, Rector of Saint Joseph Seminary, staff and seminarians, I offer my special greetings and gratitude.

Young friends, I am very happy to have the opportunity to speak with you. Please pass on my warm greetings to your family members and relatives, and to the teachers and staff of the various schools, colleges and universities you attend. I know that many people have worked hard to ensure that our gathering could take place. I am most grateful to them all. Also, I wish to acknowledge your singing to me Happy Birthday! Thank you for this moving gesture; I give you all an "A plus" for your German pronunciation! This evening I wish to share with you some thoughts about being disciples of Jesus Christ—walking in the Lord's footsteps, our own lives become a journey of hope.

In front of you are the images of six ordinary men and women who grew up to lead extraordinary lives. The Church honors them as Venerable, Blessed, or Saint: each responded to the Lord's call to a life of charity and each served him here, in the alleys, streets and suburbs of New York. I am struck by what a remarkably diverse group they are: poor and rich, lay men and women—one a wealthy wife and mother—priests and sisters, immigrants from afar, the daughter of a Mohawk warrior father and Algonquin mother, another a Haitian slave, and a Cuban intellectual.

Saint Elizabeth Ann Seton, Saint Frances Xavier Cabrini, Saint John Neumann, Blessed Kateri Tekakwitha, Venerable Pierre Toussaint, and Padre Felix Varela: any one of us could be among them, for there is no stereotype to this group, no single mold. Yet a closer look reveals that there are common elements. Inflamed with the love of Jesus, their lives became remarkable journeys of hope. For some, that meant leaving home and embarking on a pilgrim journey of thousands of miles. For each there was an act of abandonment to God, in the confidence that he is the final destination of every pilgrim. And all offered an outstretched hand of hope to those they encountered along the way, often awakening in them a life of faith. Through orphanages, schools and hospitals, by befriending the poor, the sick and the marginalized, and through the compelling witness that comes from walking humbly in the footsteps of Jesus, these six people laid open the way of faith, hope and charity to countless individuals, including perhaps your own ancestors.

And what of today? Who bears witness to the Good News of Jesus on the streets of New York, in the troubled neighborhoods of large cities, in the places where the young gather, seeking someone in whom they can trust? God is our origin and our destination, and Jesus the way. The path of that journey twists and turns—just as it did for our saints—through the joys and the trials of ordinary, everyday life: within your families, at school or college, during your recreation activities, and in your parish communities. All these places are marked by the culture in which you are growing up. As young Americans you are offered many opportunities for personal development, and you are brought up with a sense of generosity, service and fairness. Yet you do not need me to tell you that there are also difficulties: activities and mindsets which stifle hope, pathways which seem to lead to happiness and fulfillment but in fact end only in confusion and fear.

My own years as a teenager were marred by a sinister regime that thought it had all the answers; its influence grew—infiltrating schools and civic bodies, as well as politics and even religion—before it was fully recognized for the monster it was. It banished God and thus became impervious to anything true and good. Many of your grandparents and great-grandparents will have recounted the horror of the destruction that ensued. Indeed, some of them came to America precisely to escape such terror.

Let us thank God that today many people of your generation are able to enjoy the liberties which have arisen through the extension of democracy and respect for human rights. Let us thank God for all those who strive to ensure that you can grow up in an environment that nurtures what is beautiful, good, and true: your parents and grandparents, your teachers and priests, those civic leaders who seek what is right and just.

The power to destroy does, however, remain. To pretend otherwise would be to fool ourselves. Yet, it never triumphs; it is defeated. This is the essence of the hope that defines us as Christians; and the Church recalls this most dramatically during the Easter Triduum and celebrates it with great joy in the season of Easter! The One who shows us the way beyond death is the One who shows us how to overcome destruction and fear: thus it is Jesus who is the true teacher of life (cf. *Spe Salvi*, 6). His death and resurrection mean that we can say to the Father "you have restored us to life!" (*Prayer after Communion*, Good Friday). And so, just a few weeks ago, during the beautiful Easter Vigil liturgy, it was not from despair or fear that we cried out to God for our world, but with hope-filled confidence: dispel the darkness of our heart! dispel the darkness of our minds! (cf. *Prayer at the Lighting of the Easter Candle*).

What might that darkness be? What happens when people, especially the most vulnerable, encounter a clenched fist of repression or manipulation rather than a hand of hope? A first group of examples pertains to the heart. Here, the dreams and longings that young people pursue can so easily be shattered or destroyed. I am thinking of those affected by drug and substance abuse, homelessness and poverty, racism, violence, and degradation—especially of girls and women. While the causes of these problems are complex, all have in common a poisoned attitude of mind which results in people being treated as mere objects—a callousness of heart takes hold which first ignores, then ridicules, the God-given dignity of every human being. Such tragedies also point to what might have been and what could be, were there other hands— your hands—reaching out. I encourage you to invite others, especially the vulnerable and the innocent, to join you along the way of goodness and hope.

The second area of darkness—that which affects the mind—often goes unnoticed, and for this reason is particularly sinister. The manipulation of truth distorts our perception of reality, and tarnishes our imagination and aspirations. I have already mentioned the many liberties which you are fortunate enough to enjoy. The fundamental importance of freedom must be rigorously safeguarded. It is no surprise then that numerous individuals and groups vociferously claim their freedom in the public forum. Yet freedom is a delicate value. It can be misunderstood or misused so as to lead not to the happiness which we all expect it to yield, but to a dark arena of manipulation in which our understanding of self and the world becomes confused, or even distorted by those who have an ulterior agenda.

Have you noticed how often the call for freedom is made without ever referring to the truth of the human person? Some today argue that respect for freedom of the individual makes it wrong to seek truth, including the truth about what is good. In some circles to speak of truth is seen as controversial or divisive, and consequently best kept in the private sphere. And in truth's place—or better said its absence—an idea has spread which, in giving value to everything indiscriminately, claims to assure freedom and to liberate conscience. This we call relativism. But what purpose has a "freedom" which, in disregarding truth, pursues what is false or wrong? How many young people have been offered a hand which in the name of freedom or experience has led them to addiction, to moral or intellectual confusion, to hurt, to a loss of self-respect, even to despair and so tragically and sadly to the taking of their own life? Dear friends, truth is not an imposition. Nor is it simply a set of rules. It is a discovery of the One who never fails us; the One whom we can always trust. In seeking truth we come to live by belief because ultimately truth is a person: Jesus Christ. That is why authentic freedom is not an opting out. It is an opting in; nothing less than letting go of self and allowing oneself to be drawn into Christ's very being for others (cf. *Spe Salvi*, 28).

How then can we as believers help others to walk the path of freedom which brings fulfillment and lasting happiness? Let us again turn to the saints. How did their witness truly free others from the darkness of heart and mind? The answer is found in the kernel of their faith; the kernel of our faith. The Incarnation, the birth of Jesus, tells us that God does indeed find a place among us. Though the inn is full, he enters through the stable, and there are people who see his light. They recognize Herod's dark closed world for what it is, and instead follow the bright guiding star of the night sky. And what shines forth? Here you might recall the prayer uttered on the most holy night of Easter: "Father we share in the light of your glory through your Son the light of the world...inflame us with your hope!" *(Blessing of the Fire)*. And so, in solemn procession with our lighted candles we pass the light of Christ among us. It is "the light which dispels all evil, washes guilt away, restores lost innocence, brings mourners joy, casts out hatred, brings us peace, and humbles earthly pride" *(Exsultet)*. This is Christ's light at work. This is the way of the saints. It is a magnificent vision of hope—Christ's light beckons you to be guiding stars for others, walking Christ's way of forgiveness, reconciliation, humility, joy and peace.

At times, however, we are tempted to close in on ourselves, to doubt the strength of Christ's radiance, to limit the horizon of hope. Take courage! Fix your gaze on our saints. The diversity of their experience of God's presence prompts us to discover anew the breadth and depth of Christianity. Let your imaginations soar freely along the limitless expanse of the horizons of Christian discipleship. Sometimes we are looked upon as people who speak only of prohibitions. Nothing could be further from the truth! Authentic Christian discipleship is marked by a sense of wonder. We stand before the God we know and love as a friend, the vastness of his creation, and the beauty of our Christian faith.

Dear friends, the example of the saints invites us, then, to consider four essential aspects of the treasure of our faith: personal prayer and silence, liturgical prayer, charity in action, and vocations.

What matters most is that you develop your personal relationship with God. That relationship is expressed in prayer. God by his very nature speaks, hears, and replies. Indeed, Saint Paul reminds us: we can and should "pray constantly" (1 *Thess* 5:17). Far from turning in on ourselves or withdrawing from the ups and downs of life, by praying we turn towards God and through him to each other, including the marginalized and those following ways other than God's path (cf. *Spe Salvi*, 33). As the saints teach us so vividly, prayer becomes hope in action. Christ was their constant companion, with whom they conversed at every step of their journey for others.

There is another aspect of prayer which we need to remember: silent contemplation. Saint John, for example, tells us that to embrace God's revelation we must first listen, then respond by proclaiming what we have heard and seen (cf. 1 *John* 1:2–3; *Dei Verbum*, 1). Have we perhaps lost something of the art of listening? Do you leave space to hear God's whisper, calling you forth into goodness? Friends, do not be afraid of silence or stillness, listen to God, adore him in the Eucharist. Let his word shape your journey as an unfolding of holiness.

In the liturgy we find the whole Church at prayer. The word liturgy means the participation of God's people in "the work of Christ the Priest and of His Body which is the Church" (*Sacrosanctum Concilium*, 7). What is that work? First of all it refers to Christ's Passion, his Death and Resurrection, and his Ascension—what we call the Paschal Mystery. It also refers to the celebration of the liturgy itself. The two meanings are in fact inseparably linked because this "work of Jesus" is the real content of the liturgy. Through the liturgy, the "work of Jesus" is continually brought into contact with history; with our lives in order to shape them. Here we catch another glimpse of the grandeur of our Christian faith. Whenever you gather for Mass, when you go to Confession, whenever you celebrate any of the sacraments, Jesus is at work. Through the Holy Spirit, he draws you to himself, into his sacrificial love of the Father which becomes love for all. We see then that the Church's liturgy is a ministry of hope for humanity. Your faithful participation, is an active hope which helps to keep the world—saints and sinners alike—open to God; this is the truly human hope we offer everyone (cf. *Spe Salvi*, 34).

Your personal prayer, your times of silent contemplation, and your participation in the Church's liturgy, bring you closer to God and also prepare you to serve others. The saints accompanying us this evening show us that the life of faith and hope is also a life of charity. Contemplating Jesus on the Cross we see love in its most radical form. We can begin to imagine the path of love along which we must move (cf. *Deus Caritas Est*, 12). The opportunities to make this journey are abundant. Look about you with Christ's eyes, listen with his ears, feel and think with his heart and mind. Are you ready to give all as he did for truth and justice? Many of the examples of the suffering which our saints responded to with compassion are still found here in this city and beyond. And new injustices have arisen: some are complex and stem from the exploitation of the heart and manipulation of the mind; even our common habitat, the earth itself, groans under the weight of consumerist greed and irresponsible exploitation. We must listen deeply. We must respond with a renewed social action that stems from the universal love that knows no bounds. In this way, we ensure that our works of mercy and justice become hope in action for others.

Dear young people, finally I wish to share a word about vocations. First of all my thoughts go to your parents, grandparents and godparents. They have been your primary educators in the faith. By presenting you for baptism, they made it possible for you to receive the greatest gift of your life. On that day you entered into the holiness of God himself. You became adoptive sons and daughters of the Father. You were incorporated into Christ. You were made a dwelling place of his Spirit. Let us pray for mothers and fathers throughout the world, particularly those who may be struggling in any way—socially, materially, spiritually. Let us honor the vocation of matrimony and the dignity of family life. Let us always appreciate that it is in families that vocations are given life.

Gathered here at Saint Joseph Seminary, I greet the seminarians present and indeed encourage all seminarians throughout America. I am glad to know that your numbers are increasing! The People of God look to you to be holy priests, on a daily journey of conversion, inspiring in others the desire to enter more deeply into the ecclesial life of believers. I urge you to deepen your friendship with Jesus the Good Shepherd. Talk heart to heart with him. Reject any temptation to ostentation, careerism, or conceit. Strive for a pattern of life truly marked by charity, chastity and humility, in imitation of Christ, the Eternal High Priest, of whom you are to become living icons (cf. *Pastores Dabo Vobis,* 33). Dear seminarians, I pray for you daily. Remember that what counts before the Lord is to dwell in his love and to make his love shine forth for others.

Religious Sisters, Brothers and Priests contribute greatly to the mission of the Church. Their prophetic witness is marked by a profound conviction of the primacy with which the Gospel shapes Christian life and transforms society. Today, I wish to draw your attention to the positive spiritual renewal which Congregations are undertaking in relation to their charism. The word charism means a gift freely and graciously given. Charisms are bestowed by the Holy Spirit, who inspires founders and foundresses, and shapes Congregations with a subsequent spiritual heritage. The wondrous array of charisms proper to each Religious Institute is an extraordinary spiritual treasury. Indeed, the history of the Church is perhaps most beautifully portrayed through the history of her schools of spirituality, most of which stem from the saintly lives of founders and foundresses. Through the discovery of charisms, which yield such a breadth of spiritual wisdom, I am sure that some of you young people will be drawn to a life of apostolic or contemplative service. Do not be shy to speak with Religious Brothers, Sisters or Priests about the charism and spirituality of their Congregation. No perfect community exists, but it is fidelity to a founding charism, not to particular individuals, that the Lord calls you to discern. Have courage! You too can make your life a gift of self for the love of the Lord Jesus and, in him, of every member of the human family (cf. *Vita Consecrata*, 3).

Friends, again I ask you, what about today? What are you seeking? What is God whispering to you? The hope which never disappoints is Jesus Christ. The saints show us the selfless love of his way. As disciples of Christ, their extraordinary journeys unfolded within the community of hope, which is the Church. It is from within the Church that you too will find the courage and support to walk the way of the Lord. Nourished by personal prayer, prompted in silence, shaped by the Church's liturgy you will discover the particular vocation God has for you. Embrace it with joy. You are Christ's disciples today. Shine his light upon this great city and beyond. Show the world the reason for the hope that resonates within you. Tell others about the truth that sets you free. With these sentiments of great hope in you I bid you farewell, until we meet again in Sydney this July for World Youth Day! And as a pledge of my love for you and your families, I gladly impart my Apostolic Blessing.

QUERIDOS SEMINARISTAS, QUERIDOS JÓVENES:

Es para mí una gran alegría poder encontrarme con todos ustedes en el transcurso de esta visita, durante la cual he festejado también mi cumpleaños. Gracias por su acogida y por el cariño que me han demostrado.

Les animo a abrirle al Señor su corazón para que Él lo llene por completo y con el fuego de su amor lleven su Evangelio a todos los barrios de Nueva York.

La luz de la fe les impulsará a responder al mal con el bien y la santidad de vida, como lo hicieron los grandes testigos del Evangelio a lo largo de los siglos. Ustedes están llamados a continuar esa cadena de amigos de Jesús, que encontraron en su amor el gran tesoro de sus vidas. Cultiven esta amistad a través de la oración, tanto personal como litúrgica, y por medio de las obras de caridad y del compromiso por ayudar a los más necesitados. Si no lo han hecho, plantéense seriamente si el Señor les pide seguirlo de un modo radical en el ministerio sacerdotal o en la vida consagrada. No basta una relación esporádica con Cristo. Una amistad así no es tal. Cristo les quiere amigos suyos íntimos, fieles y perseverantes.

A la vez que les renuevo mi invitación a participar en la *Jornada Mundial de la Juventud en Sidney*, les aseguro mi recuerdo en la oración, en la que suplico a Dios que los haga auténticos discípulos de Cristo Resucitado. Muchas gracias.

PRAYER OF
HIS HOLINESS BENEDICT XVI
AT GROUND ZERO

GROUND ZERO, NEW YORK
Sunday, April 20, 2008

O God of love, compassion, and healing,
look on us, people of many different faiths and traditions,
who gather today at this site,
the scene of incredible violence and pain.

We ask you in your goodness
to give eternal light and peace
to all who died here—
the heroic first-responders:
our fire fighters, police officers,
emergency service workers, and Port Authority personnel,
along with all the innocent men and women
who were victims of this tragedy
simply because their work or service
brought them here on September 11, 2001.

We ask you, in your compassion
to bring healing to those

who, because of their presence here that day,
suffer from injuries and illness.
Heal, too, the pain of still-grieving families
and all who lost loved ones in this tragedy.
Give them strength to continue their lives with courage
    and hope.

We are mindful as well
of those who suffered death, injury, and loss
on the same day at the Pentagon and in Shanksville,
    Pennsylvania.
Our hearts are one with theirs
as our prayer embraces their pain and suffering.

God of peace, bring your peace to our violent world:
peace in the hearts of all men and women
and peace among the nations of the earth.
Turn to your way of love
those whose hearts and minds
are consumed with hatred.

God of understanding,
overwhelmed by the magnitude of this tragedy,
we seek your light and guidance
as we confront such terrible events.
Grant that those whose lives were spared
may live so that the lives lost here
may not have been lost in vain.
Comfort and console us,
strengthen us in hope,
and give us the wisdom and courage
to work tirelessly for a world
where true peace and love reign
among nations and in the hearts of all.

HOMILY OF HIS HOLINESS BENEDICT XVI DURING THE CELEBRATION OF THE EUCHARIST AT YANKEE STADIUM

YANKEE STADIUM, BRONX, NEW YORK
Fifth Sunday of Easter, April 20, 2008

DEAR BROTHERS AND SISTERS IN CHRIST,

In the Gospel we have just heard, Jesus tells his Apostles to put their faith in him, for he is "the way, and the truth and the life" (*John* 14:6). Christ is the way that leads to the Father, the truth which gives meaning to human existence, and the source of that life which is eternal joy with all the saints in his heavenly Kingdom. Let us take the Lord at his word! Let us renew our faith in him and put all our hope in his promises!

With this encouragement to persevere in the faith of Peter (cf. *Luke* 22:32; *Matt* 16:17), I greet all of you with great affection. I thank Cardinal Egan for his cordial words of welcome in your name. At this Mass, the Church in the United States celebrates the two hundredth anniversary of the creation of the Sees of New York, Boston, Philadelphia and Louisville from the mother See of Baltimore. The presence around this altar of the Successor of Peter, his brother

119

bishops and priests, and deacons, men and women religious, and lay faithful from throughout the fifty states of the Union, eloquently manifests our communion in the Catholic faith which comes to us from the Apostles.

Our celebration today is also a sign of the impressive growth which God has given to the Church in your country in the past two hundred years. From a small flock like that described in the first reading, the Church in America has been built up in fidelity to the twin commandment of love of God and love of neighbor. In this land of freedom and opportunity, the Church has united a widely diverse flock in the profession of the faith and, through her many educational, charitable and social works, has also contributed significantly to the growth of American society as a whole.

This great accomplishment was not without its challenges. Today's first reading, taken from the *Acts of the Apostles,* speaks of linguistic and cultural tensions already present within the earliest Church community. At the same time, it shows the power of the word of God, authoritatively proclaimed by the Apostles and received in faith, to create a unity which transcends the divisions arising from human limitations and weakness. Here we are reminded of a fundamental truth: that the Church's unity has no other basis than the Word of God, made flesh in Christ Jesus our Lord. All external signs of identity, all structures, associations and programs, valuable or even essential as they may be, ultimately exist only to support and foster the deeper unity which, in Christ, is God's indefectible gift to his Church.

The first reading also makes clear, as we see from the imposition of hands on the first deacons, that the Church's unity is "apostolic". It is a visible unity, grounded in the Apostles whom Christ chose and appointed as witnesses to his resurrection, and it is born of what the Scriptures call "the obedience of faith" (*Rom* 1:5; cf. *Acts* 6:7).

"Authority"…"obedience". To be frank, these are not easy words to speak nowadays. Words like these represent a "stumbling stone" for many of our contemporaries, especially in a society which rightly places a high value on personal freedom. Yet, in the light of our faith in Jesus Christ—"the way and the truth and the life"—we come to see the fullest meaning, value, and indeed beauty, of those words. The Gospel teaches us that true freedom, the freedom of the children of God, is found only in the self-surrender which is part of the mystery of love. Only by losing ourselves, the Lord tells us, do we truly find ourselves (cf. *Luke* 17:33). True freedom blossoms when we turn away from the burden of sin, which clouds our perceptions and weakens our resolve, and find the source of our ultimate happiness in him who is infinite love, infinite freedom, infinite life. "In his will is our peace".

Real freedom, then, is God's gracious gift, the fruit of conversion to his truth, the truth which makes us free (cf. *John* 8:32). And this freedom in truth brings in its wake a new and liberating way of seeing reality. When we put on "the mind of Christ" (cf. Phil 2:5), new horizons open before us! In the light of faith, within the communion of the Church, we also find the inspiration and strength to become a leaven of the Gospel in the world. We become the light of the world, the salt of the earth (cf. *Matt* 5:13–14), entrusted with the "apostolate" of making our own lives, and the world in which we live, conform ever more fully to God's saving plan.

This magnificent vision of a world being transformed by the liberating truth of the Gospel is reflected in the description of the Church found in today's second reading. The Apostle tells us that Christ, risen from the dead, is the keystone of a great temple which is even now rising in the Spirit. And we, the members of his body, through Baptism have become "living stones" in that temple, sharing in the life of God by grace, blessed with the freedom of the sons of God, and empowered to offer spiritual sacrifices pleasing to him (cf. 1 *Pet* 2:5). And what is this offering which we are called to make, if not to direct our every thought, word and action to the truth of the Gospel and to harness all our energies in the service of God's Kingdom? Only in this way can we build with God, on the one foundation which is Christ (cf. 1 *Cor* 3:11). Only in this way can we build something that will truly endure. Only in this way can our lives find ultimate meaning and bear lasting fruit.

Today we recall the bicentennial of a watershed in the history of the Church in the United States: its first great chapter of growth. In these two hundred years, the face of the Catholic community in your country has changed greatly. We think of the successive waves of immigrants whose traditions have so enriched the Church in America. We think of the strong faith which built up the network of churches, educational, healthcare and social institutions which have long been the hallmark of the Church in this land. We think also of those countless fathers and mothers who passed on the faith to their children, the steady ministry of the many priests who devoted their lives to the care of souls, and the incalculable contribution made by so many men and women religious, who not only taught generations of children how to read and write, but also inspired in them a lifelong desire to know God, to love him and to serve him. How many "spiritual sacrifices pleasing to God" have been offered up in these two centuries! In this land of religious liberty, Catholics found freedom not only to practice their faith, but also to participate fully in civic life, bringing their deepest moral convictions to the public square and cooperating with their neighbors in shaping a vibrant, democratic society. Today's celebration is more than an occasion of gratitude for graces received. It is also a summons to move forward with firm resolve to use wisely the blessings of freedom, in order to build a future of hope for coming generations.

"You are a chosen race, a royal priesthood, a holy nation, a people he claims for his own, to proclaim his glorious works" (1 *Pet* 2:9). These words of the Apostle Peter do not simply remind us of the dignity which is ours by God's grace; they also challenge us to an ever greater fidelity to the glorious inheritance which we have received in Christ (cf. *Eph* 1:18). They challenge us to examine our consciences, to purify our hearts, to renew our baptismal commitment to reject Satan and all his empty promises. They challenge us to be a people of joy, heralds of the unfailing hope (cf. *Rom* 5:5) born of faith in God's word, and trust in his promises.

Each day, throughout this land, you and so many of your neighbors pray to the Father in the Lord's own words: "Thy Kingdom come". This prayer needs to shape the mind and heart of every Christian in this nation. It needs to bear fruit in the way you lead your lives and in the way you build up your families and your communities. It needs to create new "settings of hope" (cf. *Spe Salvi*, 32ff.) where God's Kingdom becomes present in all its saving power.

Praying fervently for the coming of the Kingdom also means being constantly alert for the signs of its presence, and working for its growth in every sector of society. It means facing the challenges of present and future with confidence in Christ's victory and a commitment to extending his reign. It means not losing heart in the face of resistance, adversity and scandal. It means overcoming every separation between faith and life, and countering false gospels of freedom and happiness. It also means rejecting a false dichotomy between faith and political life, since, as the Second Vatican Council put it, "there is no human activity—even in secular affairs—which can be withdrawn from God's dominion" (*Lumen Gentium*, 36). It means working to enrich American society and culture with the beauty and truth of the Gospel, and never losing sight of that great hope which gives meaning and value to all the other hopes which inspire our lives.

And this, dear friends, is the particular challenge which the Successor of Saint Peter sets before you today. As "a chosen people, a royal priesthood, a holy nation", follow faithfully in the footsteps of those who have gone before you! Hasten the coming of God's Kingdom in this land! Past generations have left you an impressive legacy. In our day too, the Catholic community in this nation has been outstanding in its prophetic witness in the defense of life, in the education of the young, in care for the poor, the sick and the stranger in your midst. On these solid foundations, the future of the Church in America must even now begin to rise!

Yesterday, not far from here, I was moved by the joy, the hope and the generous love of Christ which I saw on the faces of the many young people assembled in Dunwoodie. They are the Church's future, and they deserve all the prayer and support that you can give them. And so I wish to close by adding a special word of encouragement to them. My dear young friends, like the seven men, "filled with the Spirit and wisdom" whom the Apostles charged with care for the young Church, may you step forward and take up the responsibility which your faith in Christ sets before you! May you find the courage to proclaim Christ, "the same, yesterday, and today and for ever" and the unchanging truths which have their foundation in him (cf. *Gaudium et Spes*, 10; *Heb* 13:8). These are the truths that set us free! They are the truths which alone can guarantee respect for the inalienable dignity and rights of each man, woman and child in our world—including the most defenseless of all human beings, the unborn child in the mother's womb. In a world where, as Pope John Paul II, speaking in this very place, reminded us, Lazarus continues to stand at our door (*Homily at Yankee Stadium*, October 2,

1979, No. 7), let your faith and love bear rich fruit in out-reach to the poor, the needy and those without a voice. Young men and women of America, I urge you: open your hearts to the Lord's call to follow him in the priesthood and the reli-gious life. Can there be any greater mark of love than this: to follow in the footsteps of Christ, who was willing to lay down his life for his friends (cf. *John* 15:13)?

In today's Gospel, the Lord promises his disciples that they will perform works even greater than his (cf. *John* 14:12). Dear friends, only God in his providence knows what works his grace has yet to bring forth in your lives and in the life of the Church in the United States. Yet Christ's promise fills us with sure hope. Let us now join our prayers to his, as living stones in that spiritual temple which is his one, holy, catholic and apostolic Church. Let us lift our eyes to him, for even now he is preparing for us a place in his Father's house. And empowered by his Holy Spirit, let us work with renewed zeal for the spread of his Kingdom.

"Happy are you who believe!" (cf. 1 *Pet* 2:7). Let us turn to Jesus! He alone is the way that leads to eternal hap-piness, the truth who satisfies the deepest longings of every heart, and the life who brings ever new joy and hope, to us and to our world. Amen.

QUERIDOS HERMANOS Y HERMANAS EN EL SEÑOR:

Les saludo con afecto y me alegro de celebrar esta Santa Misa para dar gracias a Dios por el bicentenario del momento en que empezó a desarrollarse la Iglesia Católica en esta Nación. Al mirar el camino de fe recorrido en estos años, no exento también de dificultades, alabamos al Señor por los frutos que la Palabra de Dios ha dado en estas tierras y le manifestamos nuestro deseo de que Cristo, Camino, Verdad y Vida, sea cada vez más conocido y amado.

Aquí, en este País de libertad, quiero proclamar con fuerza que la Palabra de Cristo no elimina nuestras aspiraciones a una vida plena y libre, sino que nos descubre nuestra verdadera dignidad de hijos de Dios y nos alienta a luchar contra todo aquello que nos esclaviza, empezando por nuestro propio egoísmo y caprichos. Al mismo tiempo, nos anima a manifestar nuestra fe a través de nuestra vida de caridad y a hacer que nuestras comunidades eclesiales sean cada día más acogedoras y fraternas.

Sobre todo a los jóvenes les confío asumir el gran reto que entraña creer en Cristo y lograr que esa fe se manifieste en una cercanía efectiva hacia los pobres. También en una respuesta generosa a las llamadas que Él sigue formulando para dejarlo todo y emprender una vida de total consagración a Dios y a la Iglesia, en la vida sacerdotal o religiosa.

Queridos hermanos y hermanas, les invito a mirar el futuro con esperanza, permitiendo que Jesús entre en sus vidas. Solamente Él es el camino que conduce a la felicidad que no acaba, la verdad que satisface las más nobles expectativas humanas y la vida colmada de gozo para bien de la Iglesia y el mundo. Que Dios les bendiga.

ADDRESS OF
HIS HOLINESS BENEDICT XVI
AT THE FAREWELL CEREMONY

JOHN FITZGERALD KENNEDY
INTERNATIONAL AIRPORT, NEW YORK
Sunday, April 20, 2008

MR. VICE-PRESIDENT,

DISTINGUISHED CIVIL AUTHORITIES,

MY BROTHER BISHOPS,

DEAR BROTHERS AND SISTERS,

The time has come for me to bid farewell to your country. These days that I have spent in the United States have been blessed with many memorable experiences of American hospitality, and I wish to express my deep appreciation to all of you for your kind welcome. It has been a joy for me to witness the faith and devotion of the Catholic community here. It was heart-warming to spend time with leaders and representatives of other Christian communities and other religions, and I renew my assurances of respect and esteem to all of you. I am grateful to President Bush for kindly coming to greet me at the start of my visit, and I thank Vice-President

Cheney for his presence here as I depart. The civic authorities, workers and volunteers in Washington and New York have given generously of their time and resources in order to ensure the smooth progress of my visit at every stage, and for this I express my profound thanks and appreciation to Mayor Adrian Fenty of Washington and Mayor Michael Bloomberg of New York.

Once again I offer prayerful good wishes to the representatives of the see of Baltimore, the first Archdiocese, and those of New York, Boston, Philadelphia and Louisville, in this jubilee year. May the Lord continue to bless you in the years ahead. To all my Brother Bishops, to Bishop DiMarzio of this Diocese of Brooklyn, and to the officers and staff of the Episcopal Conference who have contributed in so many ways to the preparation of this visit, I extend my renewed gratitude for their hard work and dedication. With great affection I greet once more the priests and religious, the deacons, the seminarians and young people, and all the faithful in the United States, and I encourage you to continue bearing joyful witness to Christ our Hope, our Risen Lord and Savior, who makes all things new and gives us life in abundance.

One of the high-points of my visit was the opportunity to address the General Assembly of the United Nations, and I thank Secretary-General Ban Ki-moon for his kind invitation and welcome. Looking back over the sixty years that have passed since the Universal Declaration of Human Rights, I give thanks for all that the Organization has been able to achieve in defending and promoting the fundamental rights of every man, woman and child throughout the world, and I encourage people of good will everywhere to continue working tirelessly to promote justice and peaceful co-existence between peoples and nations.

My visit this morning to Ground Zero will remain firmly etched in my memory, as I continue to pray for those who died and for all who suffer in consequence of the tragedy that occurred there in 2001. For all the people of America, and indeed throughout the world, I pray that the future will bring increased fraternity and solidarity, a growth in mutual respect, and a renewed trust and confidence in God, our heavenly Father.

With these words, I take my leave, I ask you to remember me in your prayers, and I assure you of my affection and friendship in the Lord. May God bless America!

REFLECTIONS ON THE PAPAL VISIT TO THE UNITED NATIONS

Most Reverend Celestino Migliore, JCD
TITULAR ARCHBISHOP OF CANOSA,
APOSTOLIC NUNCIO
PERMANENT OBSERVER MISSION OF THE
HOLY SEE TO THE UNITED NATIONS

Prior to Pope Benedict XVI's coming to the United Nations in New York, many did not expect him to make a "politically correct" speech.

For weeks, I was inundated with questions on what the Pope would say. Obviously, it was not possible to anticipate the particulars. However, the questions were quite telling indeed, for they were an indication that the words of the Pope still carry weight today, and that he would come to the United Nations not as any head of state but as a moral authority: a moral authority that fosters a plan, safeguards the founding principles, and values the life of the individual and the community; a moral authority that is recognized as "natural law," which precedes and cannot be contradicted by the laws of the state; a moral authority that uses particular means to achieve all this—persuasion and negotiation, which shun any use of force or imposition.

The Pope did not dwell—in the interest of time—on the various crises and challenges that concern the world today. Rather, he went right to the root of every problem and every solution; namely, human rights, which are based on natural law inscribed in the human heart, are present in different cultures and civilizations, and necessary for the dignity of every human person.

The Pope also stated that the moral basis for a government's claim to authority, to sovereignty, is its responsibility for, its willingness to, and its effectiveness in protecting its population from any kind of violation of human rights. While borrowing this expression from the *Outcome Document* adopted by heads of state and government in 2005, Pope Benedict outlined a broader concept. Responsibility to protect covers not only so-called humanitarian interventions, which at times require the use of force; rather, responsibility could be used as the new name for sovereignty, which is not only a right, but above all a responsibility to protect and promote the populations in their daily lives.

This is a time of difficulty and tension for the United Nations, and yet the Pope uplifted spirits. I was pleased to learn that many diplomats who heard him stress the utmost potential of the United Nations felt comforted and encouraged to work for a U.N. that *delivers*. In particular, they had the impression that the Pope was reading their hearts, their personal desires for justice and freedom. From the feedback I received from diplomats and officials at the United Nations, the words of the Pope will continue to resonate, to inspire in-depth reflections, and to be studied further, especially with regard to the role of the United Nations and international law.

In his meetings with the United Nations' personnel, he generated real enthusiasm that enveloped all, regardless of one's religious affiliation. Speaking of the United Nations as a family of nations, the Pope created a new sense of family among the thousands of workers and collaborators there. A poignant moment was when he engendered motivation and a sense of dignity by mentioning all the job positions—from translators, to ushers, to security agents—and applied to their daily work-relations the concrete awareness of the responsibility to protect and promote that which constitutes the mission of the United Nations.

REFLECTIONS ON THE PASTORAL VISIT OF OUR HOLY FATHER TO THE CHURCH IN THE UNITED STATES

Most Reverend Donald W. Wuerl, STD
ARCHBISHOP OF WASHINGTON

The apostolic journey of our Holy Father, Pope Benedict XVI, was a time of grace for the Church in the United States. The Pope's visit provided all of us an opportunity to renew our appreciation of our faith, of the role of Peter in Christ's plan for his Church, and of the continuation of that ministry in the person of Pope Benedict XVI. As he said in his homily during Mass at Nationals Park in Washington, "As the Successor of Peter, I have come to America to confirm you, my brothers and sisters, in the faith of the Apostles."

From the time of his arrival at Andrews Air Force Base on Tuesday, April 15, until his departure on Sunday, April 20, his warm and enveloping smile, his gracious kindness, and his affirming and challenging teaching inspired all of us with a vision of deep faith and unshakable hope. I have heard from so many people who are not Catholic how his presence and message affected them so positively.

The Holy Father began his homily at Nationals Park by declaring that he had "come to repeat the Apostle [Peter]'s urgent call to conversion and the forgiveness of sins, and to implore from the Lord a new outpouring of the Holy Spirit upon the Church in this country." In so much of what the Pope had to say to us, he reminded us of the outpouring of the Spirit that is the source of the new Pentecost of which we are all a part.

As part of this renewal in the Spirit, he encouraged us to remain faithful to the teachings of the Church and to be evangelizers prepared to explain the teaching to others. He said, "Here I wish to offer a special word of gratitude and encouragement to all those who have taken up the challenge of the Second Vatican Council, so often reiterated by Pope John Paul II, and committed their lives to the new evangelization....The fidelity and courage with which the Church in this country will respond to the challenges raised by an increasingly secular and materialistic culture will depend in large part upon your own fidelity in handing on the treasure of our Catholic faith."

The renewal of the Church in America, the Pope declared, must begin with interior conversion and with the cultivation of a mindset that is genuinely Catholic. We must resist cultural trends—secularism, materialism, and individualism—that too often are barriers to a vibrant dialogue between faith and public life and to resist treating faith as simply a "private matter." As he told the bishops, "Only when their faith permeates every aspect of their lives do Christians become truly open to the transforming power of the Gospel." Only then may Christians truly become a "leaven in society" and "spread the message of Christian hope throughout the world."

In his address to young people and seminarians at Saint Joseph's Seminary in New York, the Holy Father offered them—and all of us—a vision and the challenge of this life of following Christ. "Let your imaginations soar freely," he encouraged them, "along the limitless expanse of the horizons of Christian discipleship....Authentic Christian discipleship is marked by a sense of wonder. We stand before the God we know and love as a friend, the vastness of his creation, and the beauty of our Christian faith."

Perhaps the best way we can express our gratitude for the visit of the Successor of Peter to our nation is to take his joyful challenge to heart, to be renewed in our enthusiasm for our faith, and to share this love and zeal with those around us.

CNS Photo/Karen Callaway

REFLECTIONS ON THE PASTORAL VISIT OF OUR HOLY FATHER TO THE CHURCH IN THE UNITED STATES

His Eminence
Edward Cardinal Egan, JCD, DD
ARCHBISHOP OF NEW YORK

On the morning of Friday, April 18, 2008, His Holiness Pope Benedict XVI arrived in New York City to begin a three-day pastoral visit, the theme of which was hope. His first appointment was at the United Nations, where he addressed the General Assembly in an auditorium filled to overflowing with diplomats and visitors. The words of the Bishop of Rome were powerful and received with thunderous applause.

In the evening, Pope Benedict was scheduled to speak to three hundred Orthodox and Protestant clergy in Saint Joseph's Parish Church in the Yorkville section of Manhattan. What he had to say touched the hearts of all in this historic house of worship built well over a century ago by the German Catholics of New York. The same was true of his cordial and loving greetings to members of the Jewish community some minutes earlier at the Park East Synagogue, a short distance away.

On Saturday morning the Holy Father traveled along Fifth Avenue from the residence of the Permanent Observer of the Holy See, to the United Nations on 72nd Street, and then to Saint Patrick's Cathedral on 50th Street, where 3,000 priests, deacons, religious women, and religious men awaited him. At the front door, Cathedral Rector Monsignor Robert Ritchie and Mayor Michael Bloomberg of New York greeted him with great warmth, as those within the Cathedral applauded and cheered.

Never before had a Bishop of Rome celebrated Mass in Saint Patrick's. The solemnity and splendor of the ceremony will never be forgotten, as hundreds of letters assured me over the next several weeks. After the Mass, Pope Benedict and his entourage joined me and the auxiliary bishops of the archdiocese for a luncheon in my residence to celebrate the third anniversary of his election to the See of Peter. His priest-secretary and I then joined him in the Pope-mobile to return to the residence on 72nd Street, with 200,000 men, women, and children lining Fifth Avenue, waving and cheering at the top of their voices.

In the afternoon, we all made our way to the major seminary of the archdiocese, Saint Joseph's in the Dunwoodie sector of Yonkers, New York. There, in the seminary chapel, the Holy Father met and prayed with fifty disabled children, many seated in wheelchairs and all accompanied by parents and caregivers. The beauty of the encounter cannot be overstated, so gracious and loving was the Bishop of Rome. From there he was taken to a huge, grassy field on the seminary grounds fitted with a mammoth stage where popular musicians and singers had been entertaining 34,000 youth, joined by 2,500 future priests and religious. What transpired next was magic. The Vicar of Christ and his youthful flock connected immediately in a celebration of joy, prayer, and hope that captivated all who were present and all who followed the event on television and radio as well.

The final day of the Holy Father's Pastoral Visit began under cloudy skies at the scene of the tragedy of the World Trade Center. There he knelt in prayer, consoled the loved ones of victims, embraced survivors, greeted the heroes of 9/11 from the police and fire departments and from emergency services, and enthralled both the city and the world with his kindness and compassion. Happily, in the afternoon a bright sun appeared in a cloudless sky as the 264th Successor of Saint Peter entered Yankee Stadium in the Popemobile to offer the Eucharistic Sacrifice for a congregation of 59,000. As in all of his other appearances, he lifted our hearts and ignited in each of us that hope which genuine trust in Our Lord and Savior, Jesus Christ, never fails to confer.

In the evening, the Supreme Pontiff went to the John F. Kennedy Airport, where the Most Reverend Nicholas DiMarzio, Bishop of Brooklyn, had prepared a splendid ceremony of departure keynoted by Vice President Dick Cheney. As we waved goodbye, the Alitalia jet departed New York, but the wonder of the Holy Father's three days in our midst remained. "I feel that I have come to know Pope Benedict personally," one layman told me a few days later. "He is a wise and humble pastor of souls. I hope you told him that we all love him." I reported that I had and added that all who participated in his visit to New York had told him too. For their affection was clear in their cheers, in their prayers, and in the tears that filled so many eyes—tears of joy, tears of gratitude, and—yes—tears of love.

"With these words, I take my leave, I ask you to remember me in your prayers, and I assure you of my affection and friendship in the Lord. May God bless America!"

Pope Benedict XVI
Farewell Ceremony
April 20, 2008